Things God wants us to know

Things God wants us to know

Roger Carswell

Roger Carswell worked as a secondary school teacher in West Yorkshire for over ten years. He now works full-time speaking around the world to students and adults about the believability of the Christian faith and its relevance to modern life. His other books include *And Some Evangelists...* (ISBN 978-1-85792-512-8) describing the work of the evangelist. He is married to Dot and they have four children.

ISBN 978-184550-242-3

10 9 8 7 6 5 4 3 2 1

First published in 2007
by
Christian Focus Publications, Ltd.,
Geanies House, Fearn, Ross-shire,
IV20 1TW, Great Britain.

www.christianfocus.com

Cover design by Moose77.com

Printed by Nørhaven Paperback A/S

Contents

Acknowledgements

When I first understood that God had taken the initiative to reach out not only to the world, but to me, I was overjoyed. At last, God began to make sense to me, and I responded to His love, shown in Jesus, by trusting Him as Lord and Saviour. I have not regretted that moment: God has never been a disappointment.

I pray that this little book will make this wonderful truth clear to you, too.

I want to thank my mother, now in her late eighties, but whose eye for detail is undimmed. Good grammar and the comma owe their continuing existence to her. Thanks too to Emma Balch who, living in Buenos Aires, scrutinised this manuscript, and improved it.

Dedication

This book is dedicated
to

Warren and Betty Wiersbe

American author and pastor, and his wife, who first encouraged me to write, and have been faithful friends, lavishing pastoral care, friendship and cheer in my direction for many years. Their love for God, and glint in their eye, demonstrate the value of listening to the things God wants us to know.

One

Questioning our questions

'Atheism never composed a symphony. Never painted a masterpiece. Never dispelled a fear. Never healed a disease. Never gave peace of mind. Never dried a tear. Never established philanthropy. Never gave an intelligent answer to the vast mystery of the universe. Never gave meaning to man's life on earth. Never built a just and peaceful world. Never built a great and enduring civilisation.'

Charles M. Houser

On a number of occasions I have enjoyed sitting with friends, tucking into food and grappling with issues raised when we have started with the question, 'If you could ask God anything, what would it be?' It's a great discussion starter. Sometimes the topics raised are deeply personal, whilst others are quite straightforward, though genuinely felt, questions of belief. The response, though, is never dull.

There is a Middle Eastern proverb that says, 'It is more difficult to ask a good question than it is to give a good answer'. You just have to listen to a toddler and it is clear that naturally human beings ask questions, and want answers. It is how we learn. Sadly, there is a danger in our busy world that we simply live by rote. If our leisure time is consumed by soaps, soccer and stardom then there is a danger that we will cease to question anything! Could it be that some of the issues that concern us are not those highest on God's agenda? Perhaps we are missing the point even when we ask questions; so, are we thinking through the right questions? Supposing we were to ask God what He wants us to know, how would He respond? If God is there, is He silent, or does He communicate? And if He does speak, what does He want to communicate to us? What is He passionate about? What is on the mind of God? Is what concerns Him, the same as what bothers us?

Douglas Coupland's book *Life after God*, which was published in 1994, caused quite a stir. He concludes it by saying:

> Now – here is my secret:
> I tell it to you with an openness of heart that I doubt I shall ever achieve again, so I pray that you are in a quiet room as you hear these words. My secret is that I need God – that I am sick and can no longer make it alone. I need God to help me give, because I no longer seem to be capable of giving; to help me be kind, as I no longer seem capable of kindness; to help me love, as I seem beyond being able to love.

That's quite an honest admission! Christians have good reason to believe that God *is*, and that neither Douglas Coupland nor anyone else need be left in a frustrating quandary. God has not just wound up the world like a toy, and left it so that with curiosity He can watch it unwind. Rather, He is interested, involved, and even in the world that He has made. God is concerned and communicates.

I would like it to get into the mindset of art gallery security officers! When I have half a chance, I pop into galleries and am left in awe at the amazing, accurate and artistic beauty created by strokes of a brush, pen or knife, and portrayed on canvas. I could stare for ages, yet I notice the security guards sitting apparently bored and disinterested. Is that how they are supposed to be? Are they paid to look indifferent, to bite their finger nails and gaze into space? Or have they become desensitised to the value and beauty that hangs yards away from them? Likewise, I fear that many brought up in the Western countries may similarly have lost the wonder and awe of God's world and the good news of Jesus. Familiarity may have bred contempt, or at least disinterest. However, to those willing to look, there are treasures, that God wants us know, worth discovering.

It is basic to the Christian message that God has revealed Himself to the world He has made. We are often given the impression by the media that human beings are on a long search for God. Sometimes educationalists convey the idea that God is on top of a mountain, and people are making their way to him using different routes, but all going in the same direction. These may be intriguing ideas, but they are far from the God who has made Himself known.

Christians believe that the Bible is God's message to humanity; that when we open it to read, we are in effect opening the mouth of God and allowing Him to speak to us. The Bible makes it clear that men and women are not actually looking for God, but rather running away from Him. We are wanting to do our own thing.

God has made Himself known in various ways. The world, and universe around us, is wonderful. As we will see, all of creation has been ruined; but there is still something magnificent about the world in which we live. Whether it is the infinitesimally minute DNA structure that makes us as humans or the enormity of space and the billions of stars there is evidence of design, and therefore a designer. To gaze through either a microscope or a telescope is evidence that there is order, intricacy and design to all that we see. To pause and look at a delicate snowdrop which pushes itself through the hard frozen winter soil, or to wonder at a beautiful sunset, is a reminder that God is infinite in His creativity, orderly in His design, and extravagant in His provision. That is why, contrary to what is often thought, so many great scientists of the past and present have a robust Christian faith.

However, God has not only shown us that He exists, but also what He is like. He has done this through the Bible, and through the man Jesus. As well, God has been at work in history, and the lives of individual men and women, making people aware of Him, and bringing people into a personal relationship with Him.

So God has not left us in the lurch, groping in the dark to try to find truth, as the media would have us believe. He wants us to know ultimate reality; He has no desire for us to fumble through life, existing but blinkered or blinded to spiritual truth. God wants us to know about Him, and actually to know Him.

The nineteenth century poet, Elizabeth Barrett Browning's parents disapproved so strongly of her marriage to Robert that they disowned her. Almost weekly, Elizabeth wrote love letters to her mother and father, longing for everything to be sorted out between them. They never once replied. After ten years of letter writing, Elizabeth received a huge box in the mail. She opened it. To her dismay and heartbreak, the box contained all of her letters to her parents. Not one of them had ever been opened.

Today those love letters are among the most beautiful in classical English literature. Had her parents opened and read only a few of them reconciliation might have been affected. Similarly, God has spoken to us, making Himself known to the people He has made. Sadly, what He has said is often neglected or even rejected. God is there; He is not silent, but in practise He can be silenced if we refuse to listen. It is easy to do, in effect, what Elizabeth Browning's parents did, and throw God's love and message back in His face.

If we are open to God, we will find that He disturbs our presuppositions. Throughout our lives we are bombarded with our secular age's attitudes to life. Living in a post-Christian era we pick up attitudes that are antagonistic to the world view that God has made known to us. God is marginalised; conveniently kept at a distance; only to be consulted in times of trouble. We will find that God's agenda can be quite different from that of the government's, the media's or even our peers. It is amazing what we accept without ever really questioning. Jesus confronts the beliefs and behaviour, which are contrary to what is right, and that can be disturbing. As one reads the Bible, we will probably find that what it says is quite different from the view of the Bible that we were taught in Religious Education lessons years ago. It is a thrilling and exciting book, making God known to us, and focusing attention on Jesus Christ. Just the realisation through reading, that the Bible is not religious thoughts of human beings of long ago, but God vibrantly speaking to us today, is overwhelming.

God's priorities are very different from our materialistic, pleasure seeking society. But then our society offers little to those who are wondering what is the purpose of life, or to those who are grieving because they have messed up their lives, or those who have lost a loved one, or to those who are considering what happens when a person dies. The Bible does not dodge the straightforward questions of where have we come from, why are we here and where are we going. There are answers to these issues.

We discover these answers as we look at some of the themes of the Bible, examining what God wants us to know about Himself, and about ourselves. The restlessness and emptiness, which often characterises our lives, need not be the norm. In finding answers to life's biggest questions, there is freedom and joy, and it is there to be discovered.

In the Book of Proverbs in the Bible, there is a chapter where wisdom, which is the knowledge of God, is portrayed as a woman prophet preaching in places where people gather in the city. She is drawing attention to herself, like a wayward woman, but making a very different kind of offer with her encouraging invitation:

> 'Now then, my sons, listen to me; blessed are those who keep my ways. Listen to my instruction and be wise; do not ignore it. Blessed is the man who listens to me, watching daily at my doors, waiting at my doorway. For whoever finds me finds life and receives favour from the

Lord. But whoever fails to find me harms himself; all who hate me love death.'[1]

ENDNOTES

1. Proverbs 8:32-36, see also 1:21-22.

Two

God wants us to know who He is

'Who can look upon statues or paintings without thinking at once of a sculptor or painter? ... And when one enters a well-ordered city ... what else will he suppose but that this city is directed by good rulers? So he who comes to the truly Great City, this world, and beholds hills and plains teeming with animals and plants, ... the yearly seasons passing into each other, ... and the whole firmament revolving in rhythmic order, must he not ... gain the conception of the Maker and Father and Ruler also?' [1]

Philo (1st century, Jewish writer)

It is common to hear people say words like, 'My view of God is...' The problem with that sentence is that there could be six billion views of God, and they could all be wrong! The issue is not what is my view of God, but what is God's view of God? What is He really like? What has he told us about Himself?

There are others who believe that they themselves are god! The trouble with that idea is that the gods will never live up to expectations, and will die when they die! This is hardly a god worthy of worship, trust or service!

Of course, there are those who don't believe in God at all. The atheist, Richard Dawkins expressed his non-belief by describing an evolved world of 'no design, no purpose, no evil and no good, nothing but blind, pitiless indifference'.[2] But those words don't ring true and jar against what we know of ourselves. There are too many unanswered questions in Dawkins. He doesn't explain the scores of fulfilled prophecies in the Bible, nor the historical evidence for the resurrection of Jesus, or how we know what is good or bad, or the dramatic change of life, a person who trusts Jesus, experiences.

There is a deep-seated conscious awareness of something 'other' in each of us, and our hearts are restless until they find their rest in God. The people I meet instinctively know that life has a purpose. That awareness is reinforced when they witness the birth of a baby, (no father, seeing a little son or daughter emerge into the world cries, 'That's a wonderful conglomeration of chance chemicals?'). Equally, to gather around a grave to witness the burial of a loved one reminds us of the meaningfulness of life. (Who ever muttered at such a scene, "Well there goes a meaningless existence where nothing of value was achieved?). Are we really to believe that by chance something impersonal came about, and that with time it developed the things that make him/her personal, such as love, significance, hope, purpose, reasoning, beauty and a sense of right or wrong? To rob humanity of its awareness of being made in the image of God is identity fraud![3]

Try telling a mother in Africa who is striving to eek out a living for her children that there is no real meaning to life. Or try explaining to someone who has been falsely imprisoned that there never will be ultimate justice. Or try comforting parents who have just buried their little child by saying that there is no life after death. Deep down we know the atheists are wrong because God has put within us all an awareness of Him our Maker, and has gone to great lengths to reveal Himself to the world He made.

Confusion about God is sometimes caused because different religions have their own beliefs as to what their god is like. It is politically correct to say that they are all valid but their beliefs can be mutually contradictory. For example, Muslims and Jews believe in one God, Hindus have millions of gods, and Buddhists have no God. Clearly, not every religion can be true, or even helpful to the person who wants to find out about God. Religions tell us to do certain things, to be certain types of people and to adhere to certain dogmas. In contrast, Christianity says that doing and being and even adhering are not what does the trick. In fact there isn't a trick to be done! Rather there is a relationship with God to be gained, and that is established by receiving what God has been and done for us. Rather than adhering, we are encouraged to trust; to rest in what God is offering to us.

God has revealed Himself to the world that He has made. He has done so in many ways, as we will see. He wants us to know who He is and what He is like. Open the Bible anywhere, and as you read it will become apparent that God is making Himself known to us. Some of what we find is familiar. For example, we read that 'God is love'. Yet, those famous three words are revolutionary to the people who live in anguish that their god is spiteful and vindictive, needing to be pacified. Other aspects of God might be beyond our comprehension, e.g. that God is eternal, and has no beginning and never ends. But if we could understand all there was to know about almighty God, either God would not be God or we would not be human. To read the Bible is in effect to, open the lips of God and allow Him to speak to us.[4]

Now let us see what God has revealed about who He is.

First, *God is eternal* (He has no beginning and no end) and He is timeless (bigger than time and beyond time). Of course, our finite minds cannot fathom the depths of this because everything we know has a beginning and an end. C.S. Lewis answered questions that this might arouse arguing, 'It is clear that there never was a time when nothing existed; otherwise nothing would exist now.'[5] God has revealed Himself saying He is from everlasting to everlasting:[6] a thousand years are like a day in God's sight.[7]

God is a spirit.[8] It is not possible, therefore, to put God in a display cabinet or scientific laboratory to scientifically analyse him, for He cannot be seen or touched. Nevertheless, He is 'He', not in a masculine way but in a personal sense. God is a real person, who like the people He made, has emotion and senses. God can be known and enjoyed, so human beings can have a relationship with Him. He wants to be our Heavenly Father, and make us His children.

There is only one God.[9] This is made absolutely clear throughout the Bible, as God wants to steer His people away from the multiplicity of false gods and idols that the nations round about were worshipping. There is, though, multiple personality in the Godhead, so that we read of the Father, the Son and the Holy Spirit each being God. There is only one God who is in three persons. There is love, communication, submission and personality within the triune God. We will see that God is love. For that to be true there must be multiple personality within the person of God: how else would God's love have been expressed before there was anything created? In 'eternity past' the Father loved the Son, who loved the Holy Spirit, who loved the Father. There has always been love within the Godhead.

God is all-powerful.[10] He is the one who spoke and formed the universe out of nothing bringing everything into being. It is hard for us to take in the vastness of the universe. Cambridge physicist Stephen Hawking says in his best-selling *a Brief History of Time'* that our galaxy is an average-sized spiral galaxy that looks to other galaxies like a swirl in a pastry roll and that it is over 100,000 light years across – about six hundred trillion miles. He says, 'We now know that our galaxy is only one of some hundred thousand million that can be seen using modern telescopes, each galaxy itself containing some hundred thousand million stars'. It is commonly held that the average distance between these hundred thousand million galaxies (each six hundred trillion miles across and containing one hundred thousand million stars) is three million light-years! It is noteworthy that Charles Darwin himself in his autobiography and his letters, as an old man, repeatedly remarked, 'I cannot believe with my mind that all this was produced by chance.'

God is the Creator,[11] and not the creation of peoples' imagination. The idea that if there weren't a God we would have to invent one is nonsense. If there wasn't a God we would not be here to invent one! The world we inhabit must have had an origin. That origin must have consisted in a cause. That cause must have been intelligent. That intelligence must have been supreme, and that which was and is supreme we know by the name God. The Creator of the world is the owner of it. He keeps the world going, by His power, and has a purpose for all He has made.

God knows all things.[12] He understands us better than we understand ourselves. He is never surprised by anything, for the past, present and future are all known to Him. He has never thought, 'I didn't expect that!' There is never an emergency cabinet meeting in heaven, for He is never caught out unawares. He knows all the details of our lives. He weighs our secret thoughts. He knows the motives of our actions and all the machinations of our minds. He hears people using the breath that He gave them to argue against God, and He laughs at them.[13]

God is everywhere,[14] so it is impossible to hide from or escape His presence. There is no such thing as a God-forsaken spot on earth. God is infinite and is not limited by time, energy or capability.

God never changes.[15] He does not have moods. He is consistent and reliable. When He gives His word, He can be relied upon; He is trustworthy. God is eternal, without beginning or end; he cannot die.

God is totally pure and spotless.[16] Such holiness not only means that God has done no wrong or is incapable of wrong, but that He is intrinsically pure. There are angels in heaven, who themselves have never sinned, but who when entering the presence of God are over-awed by the sense of His absolute holiness.

God has never grown accustomed to wrong doing; He has never 'learned' to tolerate wrongdoing, but consistently hates sin, ungodliness and unrighteousness. He cannot excuse or overlook what is wrong, because He knows better than anyone the destruction that sin causes. He does not sit round a negotiating table compromising on what is or is not acceptable.

His standards are absolute. He is not the God of situational ethics, adjusting what is permissible according to the fads or trends of the times! Of course, if there were no God, then there could be no absolute standard of right and wrong. We might judge that the common good was an acceptable framework, but who is to determine what is good? I remember, as a teenager seeing on the news, the atheistic Communist leader Khrushchev sitting at his desk in the United Nations pounding it with his shoe and shouting, "It's wrong! It's wrong!" What a strange and inconsistent thing for an atheist to say!

Injustice is infuriating. God is absolutely just,[17] and is concerned for equity and justice. There is no partiality or unfairness in Him, so when God ultimately judges, He will judge all people according to truth. God cannot be hoodwinked; He knows all the evidence, so the judge of all the earth will always do what is right. Sin must be punished for He cannot merely overlook wrongdoing as if it does not matter. He is truth and all that is contrary to it, is against Him.

And *God is love.*[18] His love is infinite and eternal; yet, his love is focused on each individual. When God loves, He loves the world; when God gives, He gives His Son; and when God saves, He saves forever, for we read in the Bible, 'For God so loved the world that He gave His one and only Son, that whoever believes in Him should not perish, but have eternal life.'[19] God is not unmerciful, but delights in showing mercy, compassion and forgiveness to all who will turn to Him. His love is greater than friendship, or charitable love, or romantic love. They can be passionate and strong, but they can also fade and fail, whereas God's love is consistent. He loves us even when we don't love Him; He is patient. We read of Him, 'But you O Lord, are a compassionate and gracious God, slow to anger, abounding in love and faithfulness.[20]

God came into the world in the person of Jesus.[21] It was the plan of God, even before the foundation of the world, that, at the right moment, He the Creator would become like us His creation. God had no intention of turning His back on, or washing His hands of, the world He had made and loved. God would take on Himself flesh and blood. He would enter our world, coming to rescue the very people who had turned from Him and gone their own way.

The Bible explains this as 'The Father sent His Son to be the Saviour of the world.' [22] Or as a child expressed it, 'Jesus is God with skin on!' The sixteenth century German reformer Martin Luther understood that for Jesus to accomplish all that He did, He had to be God Himself. Luther wrote: 'Now, to give grace, peace, everlasting life, forgiveness of sins, to justify, to save, to deliver from death and hell, surely these are not the works of any creature, but of the sole majesty of God … We must think of no other God than Christ.'[23]

Some years ago, a few days before Christmas, I joined a team of people from a Glasgow church who go on a late night 'soup run' each Thursday. It was very cold. We set off at 10 p.m. and visited hostels, people living rough on the streets and under flyovers, as well as those who work the streets through the night. We gave them each a hot drink, soup, sandwiches and a Christmas present. A businessman, called William[24], led the team. For over fifteen years he had not missed a single Thursday night to be involved in the work.

Just after 3 a.m. we found a drunk lying on some grating near a department store. William went up to him, shook him and said, 'Jock, it's William. I have food for you.' Jock did not respond. Eventually William lay on the damp ground next to Jock, spoke face to face with the man, gave him some hot chocolate, and put the present and sandwiches in Jock's overcoat pocket.

To me, it was a thumbnail picture not only of the Christmas message, but the Christian message. God could have ignored us, in much the same way that William could have chosen to stay at home each week. Instead, God, in the person of Jesus Christ, came into this world 'to seek and to save those who are lost.' Sadly, Jock was too drunk to take much notice of William's care and kindness.

God is still at work in our world today; He communicates and is not silent. He has revealed Himself to the world that belongs to Him. The Holy Spirit is active: He holds back the world from its perilous rush to wickedness; He points people to a realistic view of themselves, and then to see Jesus as the one who can forgive and change them not only for time, but also for eternity.

Nothing could be more important than getting things right concerning God. To mistake who God is has consequences that affect the way we spend our lives, and even our eternity. There is no reason to make a mistake, because God has made Himself abundantly clear.

I recently found myself sitting opposite a nineteen year old girl whilst travelling from the north of Scotland by train to Yorkshire. We soon got into conversation and she told me her story. She comes from a broken home, but is now living with a forty year old woman. In many ways, my heart went out to the girl who had drawn such a bad deal in life. I told her about myself, and how it was I had come to know God. The questions and answers flowed as we cheerily chatted around all sorts of subjects. Eventually I gave her a copy of the Gospel of John from the Bible. She sat and read it from cover to cover, occasionally making comments like 'this is real' or 'I never knew the Bible was so interesting,' and 'All we ever got taught in R.E. at school was about other religions, not Jesus'. God speaks, and He will speak to any individual who is open to Him, through His written message to humanity, the Bible.

Endnotes

1. Philo: Special Laws, i. 6
2. *River out of Eden* published by Weidenfield and Nicolson, 1995, p. 133
3. Geoff Chapman, 'Answers in Genesis' prayer news, October – December, 2005. www.answersingenesis.org/qa
4. There is significant evidence that the Bible is God's message to humanity. Elsewhere I have summarised some of the reason why Christians believe that the Bible is God's Word. See *Why believe?* by Roger Carswell published by Authentic Media, 1990, chapter 1, 'Why believe the Bible is the Word of God'
5. *Miracles* by C.S.Lewis, published by Macmillan, 1960. Ch. 11, p 88
6. Psalm 41:13 & Isaiah 40:28
7. 2 Peter 3:8
8. John 4:24
9. Deuteronomy 6:4, Mark 12:29
10. Revelation 19:6
11. Genesis 1:1

12. Psalm 147:4
13. Psalm 2:4
14. Psalm 139:7
15. Numbers 23:19; James 1:7
16. Isaiah 6:3
17. Proverbs 24:12
18. 1 John 4:16
19. John 3:16
20. Psalm 86:15
21. John 1:1 and 14, Isaiah 9:7
22. 1 John 4:14
23. *Martin Luther: Righteous Faith* by Drew Blankman. Published by IVP, 2002, pp. 57 & 58
24. Name changed for anonymity.

Three

God wants us to know who we are

'God defend me from ever looking at a man as an animal.' [1]
Ralph Waldo Emerson

We may be infinitesimally minute compared with the size of the universe, but human beings are fearfully and wonderfully made.[2] Just as there is a sense of awe about the vastness of space, so there is inevitable wonder at the detail of the microscopically small DNA structure or the human cell. The way we human beings hold together and function is magnificent.

There is clear evidence that we have been designed, and therefore, there must be a designer. For example, think for a moment of our nervous system. Inside us are some 100,000 miles of nerve fibres along which messages shoot at speeds of 300 miles per hour. Or think of our DNA, which contains about 2,000 genes per chromosome – 1.8 metres of DNA are folded into each cell nucleus. A nucleus is six microns long. This is like putting thirty miles of fishing line into a cherry pip. And it isn't simply stuffed in. It is folded in. If folded one way, the cell becomes a skin cell. If another way, a liver cell, and so forth. To write out the information in one cell would take 300 volumes, each volume 500 pages thick. The human body contains enough DNA that if it were stretched out, it would circle the sun 260 times![3] The delicacy and intricacy with which we have been woven together demonstrates that we are not here by blind chance or accident, but have been made for a purpose, and therefore have meaning.

Each human being is special, and of immense value. I was saddened when I read in a newspaper[4] of an Australian woman, Alexia Harriton aged twenty-four, who is deaf, blind and physically and mentally disabled, wanting to sue the doctor who allowed her to be born. Her mother said that if she had known the extent of Alexia's disabilities she would have had an abortion. One sympathises hugely with both Alexia and her mother, and yet still there is a dignity and significance about human life.

The Bible expresses the awe about the wonder of the world around, and human beings in particular:

> When I consider Your heavens,
> the work of Your fingers,

the moon and the stars,
which You have set in place,
what is man that You are mindful of him,
the son of man that You care for him?
You made him a little lower than the heavenly beings
and crowned him with glory and honour.
You made him ruler over the works of Your hands;
You put everything under his feet ...[5]

Human beings have been created. At the very beginning of the Bible we have the drama of how God brought all things into being. The creation of the first man and woman was the ultimate in creation, and God delighted in what He had formed. We were made that we might know and enjoy God forever. We were made in the image of the triune God. Human beings are physical creatures. We have different colours, features, shapes and sizes, all of which make people so interesting. Just the masses of photographs in print the world over, which portray faces demonstrates how fascinating we are to each other.

But we are not merely physical creatures. We are more than bodies. We each have personality, or the soul, so that we are distinctive characters with a variety of gifts and abilities that form a fascinating kaleidoscope of energetic humanity.

However, what makes humans unique in the world is that we also have a spirit. We were made to know, appreciate, enjoy and have a relationship with God who made us. The Bible speaks about 'the whole spirit, soul and body'[6] of people, and as it states it, the spirit of a person comes first and is the most important part of our being. True humanity is about us walking in companionship with God, at one with Him in the purposes He has for the world and us.

Human beings were created with an eternal existence. Though there is a fascination with the trivia, there is an eternal dimension to humanity, which makes us ask big questions as to who we are, what we are doing and where we are going. Because the relationship with God we are created to have has been broken; we can easily feel insecure as to important truths God wants us to rest in. Henry Bowler expressed them in an 1855 painting. He portrayed a widow in her twenties leaning against a newly dug grave near to a germinating chestnut tree. Engraved on the tombstone are the words of Jesus, 'I am the resurrection and the life.' Bowler's title for the painting is, 'The doubt: Can these dry bones live?' Yet there are repeated assurances in the Bible, as well as the natural, rational sense in each of us that this life here on earth is not all there is.

We read in the Bible, 'Multitudes who sleep in the dust of the earth will awake: some to everlasting life, others to shame and everlasting contempt.'[7] It is sometimes said that nobody came back from the dead to tell us about life after death. But Jesus died, and came back. It was He who spoke most of all about heaven and hell, 'Then they will go away to eternal punishment, but the righteous to eternal life,'[8] and 'I am the Living One; I was dead, and behold I am alive for ever and ever! And I hold the keys of death and Hades (Hell).'[9] The apostle Paul spoke of Jesus saying 'Our Saviour, Christ Jesus, who has destroyed death and has brought life and immortality to light through the gospel.'[10] Each individual has an everlasting existence. It is strange then, that we are so time and earth bound that we forget that there is more to life than all we touch and see now. George Orwell once described how a wasp was sucking jam on some buttered bread on a plate. Orwell cut the wasp in half. The wasp paid no attention, but merely went on with its meal. In fact, Orwell described how the jam poured from its severed oesophagus! Only when it tried to fly away did it realise the dreadful thing that had happened to it! Human beings can be rather like the wasp, but when the time comes to 'fly away' there will be an awful realisation of the wrong priorities that have characterised so many. We are made to last forever. We will never pass our sell-by date.

The spirit, soul and body of a person together make a living being. There is inter-twining and communication between the three distinctives that make up a human being.

The greatest tragedy to hit the world occurred when the first human beings, instead of enjoying all that God had given them, rebelled against Him. They dared to defy God and shake their fist in His face refusing to accept His rule over creation. They wanted to know both evil and good, even though it would cost them dearly. The open defiance brought into the world devastation and ruin.

The close relationship between God and humans was broken, so God appeared distant to them. Sin, suffering and death would characterise what was once a truly wonderful world. Hospitals, hearses and handkerchiefs (to wipe away tears) became the norm. Men and women died spiritually, so that God seemed distant. It is as if we have been given a certificate of divorce: once there had been a happy relationship, but now there is separation and awkwardness. Eventually each individual would die in spirit, soul and body. Men and women, who had been created by God, would be cut off from Him.

The American author Mark Twain was touring Europe with his young daughter. Everywhere royalty, well-known artists and scientists honoured him. He had red-carpet treatment. Near the end of the journey, his daughter said, 'Papa, you know everyone except God, don't you?' Ouch! It is probably also true of most of us!

Ever since that disastrous moment, individuals have been born with an inherited nature that does wrong. Theologians describe this as 'original sin'. It is the nature within us that leads us to do wrong. There is something majestic about each human, but we have been wrecked by the bias to do wrong.

The early twentieth century actress Mae West in her inimitable way expressed this when she said, 'I used to be snow white, but I drifted.'[11] Actually, neither she nor we were snow white, but from the start are conceived with a nature that will lead us to do wrong.

We don't have to teach little children to tell lies, lose their temper, and be selfish or mean: they do them by nature. And the seed of sin within us sends its roots and shoots through every part of us so that we are permeated by wrongdoing. We naturally find ourselves breaking God's commandments. We neither love God with all our heart, mind, soul and strength, nor do we love others as we love ourselves. Yet Jesus said that these two commands were the summary of the Ten Commandments.

The result is that even the most respectable people are flawed; everyone is guilty of 'moments of madness'. From time to time we read of people who have laboured hard throughout their life to build themselves a good reputation and accumulate formidable skills, only to squander them over an evil obsession or an act of folly. We are all guilty before God.

Robert Louis Stevenson said, 'We all have thoughts that would shame even hell.' The Bible is even more straightforward: it says, 'There is none righteous, no not one', and 'All men are liars' and 'All have sinned and fall short of the glory of God'. In our weaker moments, we try to blame others, or our background, environment or events, but there comes a point when we have to accept the responsibility for our own wrong.

Human beings have become puzzling paradoxes, grasping after spirituality, and yet hoping to hide from God, at the self-same time.

This is not something to dismiss with a wry smile. In the Bible, we have four biographies or Gospels of Jesus: Matthew (which looks at Jesus as the King), Mark (which focuses on Jesus as a servant), Luke (seeing Jesus as the Saviour) and John (which concentrates on Jesus as the Son of God). It is in John's Gospel that we read,

> For God did not send His Son into the world to condemn the world, but to save the world through Him. Whoever believes in Him is not condemned, but whoever does not believe stands condemned already because He has not believed in the name of God's only Son. This is the verdict: Light has come into the world, but men loved darkness instead of light because their deeds were evil.[12]

It isn't comfortable reading, but it is clear that we could not be in a more serious situation.

The apostle Paul was a brilliant and deeply religious Jewish scholar at the time of Jesus. He was disciplined and devout in his religious duties. As Christianity started spreading, after the death and resurrection of

Jesus, Paul was bitterly opposed to this new religion. Zealously, and bitterly, he persecuted the followers of Jesus until his dramatic conversion to Jesus Christ on the road to Damascus.[13] Later, it was Paul who wrote much of our New Testament part of the Bible (that part of the Bible written after Jesus' life, death, resurrection and ascension back to heaven). He wrote to Christians in the city of Rome, which he had not at that time visited, and he clearly explained the gospel message to them in the great book we call 'Romans'. In the book he explains that God cannot simply wink at the sin in the lives of people. Paul, who knew how to write in a gripping way, did not easily repeat himself, but in this letter he speaks of God's wrath against sin eight times.[14]

We need to be made right with God, so that the condemnation that is ours might be removed from us. Jesus came to do this for us. We didn't ask Him to, but He did so out of sheer love for us.

Endnotes

1. *The Book of Unusual Quotations*, edited by Rudolf Flesch, Cassell, 1959
2. Psalm 139:4
3. Information from Dr. John Medina, genetic engineer, University of Washington, in 1995 lecture at Multnomah Bible College, Portland, Oregon.
4. *Daily Telegraph* 11/11/2005
5. Psalm 8:3-6
6. 1 Thessalonians 5:22
7. Daniel 12:2
8. Matthew 25:46
9. Revelation 1:18
10. 2 Timothy 1:10

11. Taken from an Icon card (www.icon-art.com)
12. John 3:17-19
13. See Acts 9
14. Romans 1:18; 2:5, 8; 3:5; 4:15; 5:9; 9:22 and 12:19

FOUR

He wants us to know what He has done

'It costs God nothing, so far as we know, to create nice things; but to convert rebellious wills cost Him crucifixion.'[1]

C.S. Lewis

God has not made the world and left it to its own devices. Rather, He is passionate about all that He has created, and wants us to know what He has done. He wants us to enter into the joy of knowing him, which He has gone to infinite lengths to bring about.

Similarly, Christian people want others to know what God has done for them. I heard the story of a minister of a church who made an appointment to meet the editor of his local newspaper. Ushered into the executive suite, the minister introduced the reason for the visit by saying, 'Sir, I am here to ask you to become a Christian!' The editor walked to window overlooking the city that the newspaper served. Standing, he paused silently for some time, then turned and said, 'Thank you for your concern. Since I was a young boy at my mother's knee not a single relation or business associate has ever taken an interest in my soul.' God is interested in the soul, and in every aspect of each individual.

The master theme of the Bible is the unfolding drama of how God would devise means whereby we, who should be banished from His presence, could be drawn back into a relationship with Him. The focus is on Jesus Christ.

The Bible first of all looks forward to His coming, then describes it, and after that applies what Jesus has done to the church, the world and individual Christians. The apostle Paul, who wrote much of our New Testament, explained Jesus' mission. As far as He was concerned, it is as if Jesus came into the world to do just three days' work. It commenced when He was nailed to the cross, and culminated when He rose again from the dead. Paul rarely or never discussed the life of Jesus. There is little mention of Jesus' virgin birth, His temptations or miracles, His sermons, or His agonising prayer in the Garden of Gethsemene prior to His crucifixion. Jesus Christ came primarily not to preach the gospel, but that there might be a gospel to preach!

The four Gospels in the New Testament, describe Jesus' amazing birth, life, ministry and teaching. To read Matthew, Mark, Luke and John is to allow Jesus to introduce Himself to us. It is as if He walks off the pages of the Bible, and invites us to meet Him.

Matthew and Luke tell us the Christmas story of Jesus' birth in the manger in Bethlehem. Though it is all too familiar in the West, it is such an enchanting story: the stable scene because there was no room in the inn, the angels announcing to shepherds the birth of 'the Saviour who is Christ the Lord' and their response, 'Let us go to Bethlehem and see this thing that has happened, which the Lord has told us about.' Then there is the visit of the wise men from the east, bringing gifts with them, and Herod's genocide against the babies of Bethlehem.

Its appeal as a story aside, its significance is that God was entering our world. The Creator was becoming like us, His creation. The opening of John's Gospel reads, 'In the beginning was the Word, and the Word was with God, and the Word was God …The Word became flesh and made His dwelling among us.'[2]

At Christmas, a junior school in Barnsley, South Yorkshire, was having a traditional school nativity play. Old people and parents had gathered into the school hall. Everything was going well until the wise men appeared all dressed up in their dressing gowns and tinfoil crowns. The first two had said their lines, moved across stage and presented to the doll in the manger the gold and then the frankincense. However, when the third wise man with his gift of myrrh noticed his parents in the audience, his mouth fell open, and over-awed, he forgot his lines! At least he had sufficient presence of mind to keep moving. Slowly, the boy knelt by the manger to present his gift, but he could not remember what to say. The teacher in the wings whispered, 'Say something.' Still no words came. 'Say anything' the teacher said in desperation. The young actor looked in the manger, and then in a broad Yorkshire accent, said the only words he knew to say to a baby: 'Eeh, he's just like his dad!' The audience roared with laughter, but the boy was absolutely right. The baby Jesus born in Bethlehem is, as the Bible puts it, the image of the invisible God.[3]

God was big enough to become small, and strong enough to become weak. God, whom the heavens cannot contain, clothed Himself with humanity. He took on Himself flesh and bones and blood. Without laying aside His deity, God became a man. He was born of the virgin Mary; born of both humanity and deity. Jesus is fully God – as much God as God is God; and fully human – as much man as man is man. He is the God-man. He is not just God indwelling a man; there have been plenty of examples of such people. Jesus is not a man deified; such men are in the realm of myths and pagan systems of thought. Jesus is both God and man, combining in one personality the two natures.

Jesus (the name means 'Saviour') came into the world to reconcile us to God. 'For God was pleased to have all His fullness dwell in Him, and through Him to reconcile to Himself all things, whether things on earth or things in heaven, by making peace through His blood, shed on the cross.'[4]

After twenty centuries, Jesus remains the greatest man in history. Born in poverty and obscurity, as a youngster He was taken as a refugee to become an asylum seeker in Egypt. He received no formal education and worked as a labourer. He never wrote a book, or a song. Jesus formally preached and ministered for only three years, without travelling far. He never spoke to flatter the authorities, and refused to compromise His message to please His audience.

In those three years of public work, He made blind people see, the mute He enabled to speak, the deaf He made to hear, and He healed lepers and lame people. On two occasions He fed thousands of hungry people with a few loaves and fishes. He spoke to and calmed in an instant the rough storm at sea. He walked on water, dispelling the fear of terrified fishermen. Jesus Christ gave dignity to women, respect to the disabled, significance to children, credibility to the family and status to each individual. He called Himself 'the Friend of sinners' and forgave people their sins saying, 'the Son of Man has authority on earth to forgive sins'.[5] Explaining this statement Jesus said, 'It is not the healthy who need a doctor, but the sick. I have not come to call the righteous, but sinners.'[6]

Nobody spoke as Jesus did: He had authority. He gave to the world the highest moral standard, preaching only what He practised. So when Jesus commanded that we should love our enemies, do good to those who hate us, bless those who curse us, pray for those who ill-treat us, turn the other cheek or go the extra mile, He was telling us to do what He Himself had been living out. His word and His works never contradicted each other. There is no sham, spin or hypocrisy about what Jesus said. His teaching and His life have never been surpassed.

It is impossible to fault the life of Jesus. Judas Iscariot, the disciple who sold Jesus for thirty pieces of silver, the price of a slave, tragically committed suicide crying, 'I have betrayed innocent blood.' Pontius Pilate, the governor who ordered Jesus to be crucified tried to appease the crowd who were braying for Jesus' death, by asking, 'Why what evil has He done? I find no fault with Him.' The criminal crucified next to Jesus said of Him, 'This man has done nothing wrong.' And the Roman soldier responsible for ensuring Jesus really was dead, said, 'Surely this man was the Son of God'. Jesus' disciple Peter, who was always an activitist said of Him, 'He *did* no sin;' John, who was very close to Jesus, said '*In* Him was no sin;' the great intellect Paul said, 'He *knew* no sin' and elsewhere we read, 'He was *without* sin.'

Throughout the time of Jesus' public teaching, He spoke saying that He would be crucified. It was the purpose of God the Father, Son and Holy Spirit that, at just the right moment in history, Jesus would come to this earth to go to the cross to deal with sin. This had been prophesied throughout the Old Testament, as prophets anticipated the coming Christ's death. The King of Israel, David writing 1,000 years before Jesus[7], and the prophet Isaiah[8] give a detailed description of how the suffering servant would carry on Himself the sin of the world. Isaiah wrote:

> Surely He took up our infirmities and carried our sorrows, yet we considered Him stricken by God, smitten by Him, and afflicted. But He was pierced for our transgressions, He was crushed for our iniquities; the punishment that brought us peace was upon Him, and by His wounds we are healed. We all, like sheep, have gone astray, each of us has turned to his own way; and the Lord has laid on Him the iniquity of us all. He was oppressed and afflicted, yet He did not open His mouth; He was led like a lamb to the slaughter, and as a sheep before her shearers is silent, so He did not open His mouth.[9]

C.S. Lewis was the professor of Mediaeval English Literature at Cambridge University. He was converted to Christ from atheism, whilst at Oxford, and is famed for writing the children's Narnia books. Whatever C.S. Lewis' intentions in writing *The Lion, the Witch and the Wardrobe,* he drew a similarity between Aslan, who is a lion, and Jesus.

The land of Narnia was a land of winter, but it was never Christmas. That was until the majestic lion, Aslan, allowed himself to be slain, and then to rise again. When Susan, one of the children in the book, understood about the lion she was shocked and asked, 'Is he – quite safe?' The answer is very apt:

> Mr. Beaver tells her more: 'Safe? ... Who said anything about safe? Course he isn't safe. But he is good. He's the King, I tell you.'

The good King Jesus was taken and stripped naked before being beaten and humiliated. He was treated unfairly in a series of mock trials, and sentenced to be executed by crucifixion, even though his judge could find no fault in Him. He was crucified between two thieves. In the hours of terrible suffering, Jesus carried on Himself the sin of the world, the purpose of His coming to earth. Jesus came to pay the penalty of the wrong of which we are guilty. He, the eternal Son of God, took the weight of the sin of the world on Himself. Jesus Himself said, 'The Son of Man came not to be served, but to serve and to give His life a ransom for many.' The disciple of Jesus, Peter, as an old man, wrote letters to Christians scattered throughout the world saturating all he said with references to the cross of Jesus.[10] He said, 'For Christ died for sinners once for all, the righteous for the unrighteous, to bring us to God. He was put to death in the body but made alive by the Spirit.'[11] John, the youngest of Jesus' twelve disciples wrote, 'The blood of Jesus (God's) Son, purifies us from all sin.'[12] And the apostle Paul wrote, 'You see, at just the right time, when we were still powerless, Christ died for the ungodly … But God demonstrates His own love for us in this: While we were still sinners, Christ died for us.'[13]

I remember once looking out of a university window into a bustling London street. Traffic wardens seemed very busy and I pondered on how a car driver could go through life without ever having to pay a parking fine. There were two possibilities. Either you make sure that you never park wrongly. However, that seems an impossible task for most, and certainly for me! There will always be an occasion when a mistake is made resulting in the parking ticket being attached to the windscreen. The other way is to find somebody who is willing to pay your fines in your place! If that sounds too good to be true, it is only an illustration of what Jesus has done for us. He has paid the price, satisfying the justice of God, whilst out of love for us Jesus carried our sins on Himself.

To enjoy a right relationship with God, who is absolutely righteous, sin has to be taken care of; it cannot be overlooked. God demonstrated His own righteousness by providing Jesus, a perfect, permanent and completely satisfactory sacrifice for sin. Through Jesus we can be made 'at one' with God.

Jesus was taken down from the cross and laid in a previously unused tomb. It was sealed with a huge stone placed in front of it, and guarded by soldiers. There Jesus lay for three days and two nights. On the first Easter Sunday morning, the stone rolled away, not so much to let Jesus out, but to let people look in and see that He had risen from the dead. He did what no religious or political leader or ordinary individual has ever done. He conquered death and sin by coming back to life.

The Killing Fields is an unforgettable film telling the true story of a New York Times reporter who was working in Cambodia and was captured by the Marxist regime, the Khmer Rouge, which was a totalitarian group known for its torturous cruelty. What this man endured while trying to find freedom is beyond belief; he was brutally beaten, imprisoned and mistreated. In his escape, he runs from one tragic situation to another. On one occasion he sinks into a bog only to discover it is a watery bog full of rotting flesh and human bones and skulls that foam to the top as he scrambles to climb out.

Having endured the rigours of the jungle while being chased by his captors, he finally steps out into a clearing and looks down. To his amazement he sees the Cambodian border, a small refugee camp, a hospital and a flag on which is a cross. At that moment the music builds to a climax, as light returns to his face, which seems to shout out, 'I'm free. I'm free!'

Jesus' work was accomplished that we might be made free. Not the freedom to do as we want, but the freedom to do what is right. He came that there might be forgiveness and new, eternal life for those who will trust Him as Lord, Saviour and Friend. We humans so often feel the need to do something to prove ourselves to God, but that is not what God wants. We need to accept within our minds and hearts the truth of God's work on our behalf, and simply receive it. Nothing more can be added to what Jesus had done on the cross for us. He alone can set us free from the slavery of following our selfish whims.

Endnotes

1. *Mere Christianity* by C.S. Lewis, published by MacMillan, 1952, p. 179
2. John 1:1 and 14
3. Colossians 1:15
4. Colossians 1:19-20
5. Mark 2:10
6. Mark 2:17
7. See Psalm 22
8. See Isaiah 53
9. Isaiah 53:4-7
10. 1 Peter 1:2; 1:11; 1:19; 2:7; 2:21 and 24; 3:18; 4:1; 4:13 and 5:1
11. 1 Peter 3:18
12. 1 John 1:7
13. Romans 5:6 and 8

God wants us to know what we must do

'To make a man happy as a lark, might be to do him grievous wrong; to make a man wake, rise, look up, turn, is worth the life and death of the Son of the Eternal.'[1]

George MacDonald
(19th century Scottish novelist and poet)

When Jesus was asked the question, 'What must we do that we may work the works of God?' He gave a startling and unexpected answer. His reply was, 'This is the work of God, that you may believe in Him whom He sent.'[2] In other words, Jesus did not speak of the good deeds we have to do, but spoke of the need for belief and trust in Him. Belief in Jesus is not the issue on which the media focuses, they are concerned with whether politically we move to the left or right. There is much to strive towards, to bring justice, economic and environmental security and an end to conflict in our world, but there are also issues of eternity, of our relationship with God and of heaven and hell. These are sorted out not by striving but by receiving what God wants to give. The infinite God can fully give Himself to everyone who will ask.

The poet Louise Tarkington expressed thoughts that many have:

> I wish there were some wonderful place
> In the land of Beginning Again
> Where all our mistakes and all our heartaches
> And all our poor selfish grief
> Could be dropped like a shabby old coat at the door
> And never put on again.

God offers to a world that has lost its bearings, a completely new start. There is a new beginning for the person who will turn in repentance, and trust Christ as Lord and Saviour. The Bible says, 'Therefore, if anyone is in Christ, he is a new creation; the old has gone, the new has come!'[3] God is willing to forgive a person all that is wrong, and give to them His righteousness, so he or she can be acceptable in His sight. Because Jesus has died and risen from the dead, we can be reconciled to His Father, God.

There was an occasion when a religious leader, called Nicodemus, came to Jesus at night time, wanting to know who Jesus really was. In the subsequent conversation, Jesus said to him, 'You must born again.'[4] We have been born once, but Jesus said we need to be born from above by the Spirit of God. It is the Holy Spirit who works in our minds to show us that we are not the people we were created to be, and then to point our attention to Jesus who loved us and gave Himself for us. God wants to work this miracle in our lives. When He does, the Holy Spirit Himself comes to live within us, and will never leave or forsake us. Our beings become God's possession, the very dwelling place of God. We can know God guiding, guarding and governing our lives through life, death and into eternity.

Anne Brontë, in her book, *The Tenant of Wildfell Hall* tells the story of Helen and the inner turmoil that she, a moral Christian woman, struggles with because of her drunken husband who is given to cruelty and immorality. Loyalty wins the day, but self-abuse takes her husband's life. His dying words to her were, 'Oh Helen, I wish you could come with me to plead for me.' Once a person has Christ as Lord and Saviour, they have Jesus to plead their cause before the Father who is in heaven. Jesus is the mediator between God and men; He is the advocate. He is the one who will take us through life's journey, to be with Him forever. None of us is good enough for God or for heaven. Yet those who belong and have become the children of God, are promised forgiveness and eternal life with Him.

One New Year's Eve I found myself unable to sleep. About three o'clock in the morning I got out of bed and leaned against the windowsill to watch the stillness of our little cul-de-sac in the early hours of a new day. We were thick in snow, and a blizzard was still blowing. Then from the nearby woods emerged a beautiful red fox. It sniffed around a number of neighbours' gardens before wandering around ours. The next morning, I went to examine the fox tracks. To my disappointment, they had all disappeared – all covered by the fresh snow, which had continued to fall throughout the night. Musing on the incident, I couldn't help thinking that all my sins could be completely covered, never to be uncovered. It would not be snow that removed my guilt, but as the Bible puts it: 'The blood of Jesus, (God's) Son, purifies us from all sin,'[5] and 'If we confess our sins, He is faithful and just, and will forgive us our sins and purify us from all unrighteousness.'[6]

God wants us to know how we can have the certainty that we are eternally secure with Him. It is not presumptuous to be sure of heaven. The Bible promises it to those who have come to the point when they have deliberately turned from their sin and ask Jesus Christ to be their Lord and Saviour. Here are some Bible quotations that state clearly that we can *know* we are safe in God's keeping, not because of anything we have done, but entirely because of what God has done in forgiving us and making us His children:

'Come now, let us reason together,' says the Lord, "Though your sins are like scarlet they shall be as white as snow; though they are red as crimson, they shall be like wool.'[7]

He saved us, not because of righteous things we had done but because of His mercy. He saved us through the washing of rebirth and renewal by the Holy Spirit.[8]

For it is by grace you have been saved, through faith – and this not from yourselves, it is the gift of God – not by works, so that on-one can boast. For we are God's workmanship, created in Christ Jesus to do good works, which God prepared in advance for us to do.[9]

Yet all who received Him, to those who believed in His name, He gave the right to become children of God – children born not of natural descent, nor of human decision or a husband's will, but born of God.[10]

He who has the Son has life; he who does not have the Son of God does not have life. I write these things to you who believe in the name of the Son of God so that you may know that you have eternal life.[11]

Jesus said, 'Assuredly, I say to you, unless you are converted and become as little children, you will by no means enter the kingdom of heaven.'[12]

How then is a person converted to Jesus Christ? How does someone put his or her faith in Jesus? It is rather like getting married. Two people, make deliberate vows to each other that forsaking all others they commit themselves to the one they love. They use simple words like 'I do' and 'I will', but those words change their whole personal standing. They then go and live out their married lives together. In a similar way, we bring words to God. We don't have to be in a church or religious setting, but from the heart to pray to God,

- thanking God for who He is and what He has done
- confessing to Him our sin and asking Him for forgiveness, because of Jesus' death and resurrection
- asking Him, by His Holy Spirit, to come to live within our life as Lord and Friend.

God hears such a prayer, and promises to answer: as we read that 'whoever calls on the name of the Lord will be saved.'[13] When God has gone to such great lengths to reach and rescue us, it is right that we should respond to His love by receiving Him, and all He has to give. Many have found it very helpful to express their faith and commitment using a prayer with words like these:

Dear God, Thank you that you have revealed Yourself to this world. Thank You for giving me life, and for showing yourself to me. I confess to you all my sin, and with Your help I want to turn from it. I ask, that because of Jesus, you would forgive me. I want Him to become my Lord, my Saviour and Friend forever. Help me to follow You and grow to become a strong Christian. Thank you for loving me, and hearing this prayer, which I pray in the name of Jesus. Amen.

It really is important to come to the moment in life where one turns to God from living one's own sinful, selfish life. The Bible calls this turning from sin, repentance.

It is crucial to trust Jesus in order to receive forgiveness and a new life, with Him as Lord and Saviour. The Bible calls that trust, believing, or faith.

In the Old Testament, there is a beautiful little love song, called the Song of Solomon which describes the relationship between a man and his lover. It shows how God made us man and woman, and how He honours love and sex. But there is a sad scene in the book where the girl has gone to her room for the night. She has anointed herself with perfumes, and retired to her bed. Then there is a knock at her door; she knows that her lover has arrived. Though she wants to be with him, she hesitates, and doesn't respond. She muses on the thought that she has now gone to bed, and she doesn't want to get up. Then, suddenly, he leaves, and cannot be found. She realises that all the perfume is absolutely worthless now the lover has gone.

It would be sad, if in a similar way, when God has revealed Himself to us, knocking on the door of our lives, he should be ignored or shunned. The obvious response is to invite Him into our lives, to trust Him and enjoy Him forever.

When one truly trusts God in this way it is the beginning of a whole new life. It is the new birth Jesus spoke about. God takes us at our word, and gives His word that we will be accepted in Christ. We are then at the start of the whole new adventure of living life with and for the Lord Jesus. God, by His Holy Spirit, comes to live within us, so that we become the dwelling place of God. It is amazing that God cleans us up by forgiving us, and giving us Himself. He will never leave, but will take us through life's journey to be with Himself forever. Carefully read these words from the Bible. They were written in the first century to encourage Christians living in the heart of the Roman Empire, which was so antagonistic to the Christian message:

> If God is for us, who can be against us? He who did not spare His own Son, but gave Him up for us all – how will He not also, along with Him, graciously give us all things? Who will bring any charge against those whom God has chosen? It is God who justifies. Who is he that condemns? Christ Jesus, who died – more that that, who

> was raised to life – is at the right hand of God, and is also interceding for us. Who shall separate us from the love of Christ? Shall trouble or hardship or persecution or famine or nakedness or danger or sword? As it is written:
>
> 'For your sake we face death all day long;
> we are considered as sheep to be slaughtered.'
>
> No, in all these things we are more than conquerors through Him who loved us. For I am convinced that neither death nor life, neither angels nor demons, neither the present nor the future, nor any powers, neither height nor depth, nor anything else in all creation, will be able to separate us from the love of God that is in Christ Jesus our Lord.[14]

God has given us help so that we can start to grow in our faith and knowledge of God. The Holy Spirit, now living within us will give us the strength to start living as we should. We know what that is by reading the Bible, which is God's word to us, in written form. I recommend the habit of spending some time with God each day, preferably without any exceptions. Let it become a daily, dogged, delightful discipline to set aside time each day to read God's word, and enjoying your relationship with God. Start by working through the New Testament. If you can buy a modern version of the Bible, whose print is not too small, it definitely helps! Don't worry if you don't understand everything. God will speak through His written word, to you. He will give you the desire and power to do all that He commands.

There are also some very helpful Bible aids to help you in your reading.[15] You will find that the Bible will become quite exciting to read, as you learn what God has said, and how different it often is to the agenda that the world is obsessed with. One man, centuries ago said, 'My greatest delight is to be in a nook, with *the* Book!'

Just as you listen to God speaking and teaching you, through reading the Bible, you can speak to Him by praying. Learn to thank and praise Him. The great scientist, Sir Isaac Newton said, 'I can take my telescope and look millions of miles into space; but I can go away to my room, and in prayer get nearer to God and heaven than I can when assisted by all the telescopes of earth.' Reading the Psalms in the Bible can help us in knowing how to praise God. Confess your sins to Him. Simply because you have become a Christian doesn't mean that you will be temptation-free or perfect overnight! Every Christian struggles against real temptations to do wrong. We are reminded that the things which satisfy our wrong desires, and the pleasures of this world, pass away, but that the person who does the will of God lives forever.[16] You can pray for others: your family, friends, Church, government, world situations, etc.

As well, God invites you to ask Him to help, guide and use you. Jesus said, 'Come to Me, all you who are weary and burdened, and I will give you rest. Take my yoke upon you and learn from Me, for I am gentle and humble in heart, and you will find rest for your souls. For My yoke is easy and My burden is light.'[17]

Church is a great place to start to grow in your Christian faith. When you become a child of God, you become part of His family. Church is where you can share worship, serve God, and witness to your faith with fellow believers. Of course, no church is perfect, for it is a collection of sinners who are gathering together. However, it is vital that you make sure your church is one where the Bible is believed and preached; where Jesus is the focus, and is loved and served; and where there are people who will care for you spiritually, and with whom you can tell others the good news of Jesus.

Sharing with others, who God is and what He has done for you, is a way in which we can show that we love God and want others to know Him too. Ask God to give you the courage to tell those you know or meet about Him. You don't need to be an oddball to winsomely share the most wonderful relationship you have with God, through Jesus.

None of these things makes us Christians, or earn us favour with God. Rather, they grow out of love for God after all He has done for us. We demonstrate that we love God by the things we do, but we enter into an eternal relationship with God, through what He has done.

God wants us to know this. And He wants everyone else to know it too!

Endnotes

1. *Unspoken Sermons* (Series Two), by George MacDonald. London: Longmans, Green, and Co., 1891.
2. John 6:28-29
3. 2 Corinthians 5:17
4. John 3:1-15
5. 1 John 1:7
6. 1 John 1: 9
7. Isaiah 1:18
8. Titus 3:5
9. Ephesians 2:8-10
10. John 1:12-13
11. 1 John 5:12-13
12. Matthew 18:3 (New King James Version)
13. Romans 10:13
14. Romans 8:31-39
15. *Our Daily Bread*, with daily readings and notes, is available from Radio Bible Class, Box 1, Carnforth, Lancashire, LA5 9ES, England.
    Explore is a quarterly book of Bible reading notes available from The Good Book Company; email: admin@thegoodbook.co.uk
    To really dig into the whole Bible over three years, I recommend *Search the Scriptures*, edited by Alan M. Stibbs, published by IVP
16. 1 John 2:15-17
17. Matthew 11:28-30

FAITHFUL SERVICE AND DIVINE FRIENDSHIP

And the Scripture was fulfilled which says, "Abraham believed God, and it was accounted to him for righteousness." And he was called the friend of God.

—JAMES 2:23

God was confirming His rhema word to me through His *logos*, the Bible. Pastor Larry Randolph's words came back to me:

> God will tell you things about people that you'll never tell other people. You'll pray and intercede, and hold them up in prayer because you're going to be a friend of God—and that's a true prophet; it's just a friend of God. He will tell you secrets about other people's lives and about things He's doing in the earth. So get ready for a fresh anointing of the prophetic to come upon your life.

Now it was happening, and I could hardly wait to discover what God would tell me next.

O Lord, my desire is to be Your faithful servant, leading on to friendship with the God of creation, whom I worship with all my heart . . .

Day 5

Heavenly Father, I thank You not only for hearing and answering prayer, but for giving us words of praise and thanksgiving until our hearts overflow with Your goodness . . .

TO PRAY IN HIS WILL

Now this is the confidence that we have in Him, that if we ask anything according to His will, He hears us. And if we know that He hears us, whatever we ask, we know that we have the petitions that we have asked of Him.

—1 JOHN 5:14–15

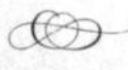

I now knew what I had once only believed—that Jesus hears and answers prayer. I had prayed that God would help me serve Him so I would not be embarrassed when I stand before Him.

I had told Him, so many times, how much I wanted to serve Him, and I always told Him that I didn't quite know how.

I now know the truth of this wonderful prayer promise. It is an infallible truth of the Word of God—that He does hear us when we pray according to His will. And His will is revealed in the Bible.

PEACE OF NO BOUNDS

Peace I leave with you, My peace I give to you; not as the world gives do I give to you. Let not your heart be troubled, neither let it be afraid.

—JOHN 14:27

"Daughter, I want you to look at something." In the spirit He transported me to an unknown church—a very large church filled with dark-skinned men. There were no women present in this particular assembly. Jesus explained, "You will visit many churches as you do My work."

After this I knew that each visit thereafter would provide me with new clues about my future. When the Lord told me that I would never have to worry again, I rejoiced. He was healing me on the inside while He prepared me for ministry.

The sweetness of His presence can only be described as total peace. It enabled me to live and walk in the truth of His Word.

Dear Lord,
may my praise of You be as wide as the pathways of Your love, as deep as the limitless peace You pour out upon me . . .

O Lord, may my joy truly be the joy of Your presence, the laughter of Your heart, the infinite beauty of the song You inspire from lips that praise You always . . .

THE LAUGHTER OF GOD

When the LORD brought back the captivity of Zion, we were like those who dream. Then our mouth was filled with laughter, and our tongue with singing. Then they said among the nations, "The LORD has done great things for them." The LORD has done great things for us, and we are glad."

—PSALM 126:1–3

Nehemiah proclaimed, "The joy of the LORD is your strength" (Neh. 8:10), and the Book of Proverbs declares, "A merry heart does good, like medicine" (Prov. 17:22). Now I know the true meaning of these healing words.

Day 8

Father, into Your hands I place all my doubts, my fears, and my misgivings, that my faith in You might yield a bond of trust so powerful it can never be broken, never strained or stretched except as You direct for building up my love and adoration...

TO HIM WHO IS ABLE

I will say of the L*ORD*, *"He is my refuge and my fortress; my God, in Him I will trust."*

—PSALM 91:2

The way the Lord addressed me as "My daughter" always brought tears of joy and love. He was so different from my earthly father. The Lord was tender, respectful, encouraging, and sensitive in all His dealings. I knew that He knew my needs before I expressed them. I knew that He was my safe place—my "Rock of refuge"—and that, compared with Him, any other "refuge" was sinking sand.

His visits, my time in prayer and the Word, the precious moments of worship at my church—all these were having deeply revolutionizing effects in my life. My faith was growing at an accelerating pace. I knew, beyond all doubt, that He is able...

Day 9

Dear Jesus, my love for You so far exceeds what I thought possible that I stand in awe and amazement. Yet even this is but a tiny foretaste of the love I know You have for me . . .

LOVE SURPASSING

There is no fear in love; but perfect love casts out fear, because fear involves torment. But he who fears has not been made perfect in love. We love Him because He first loved us.

—1 JOHN 4:18–19

His sweet voice turned my fear into laughter. I heard the echoes of His own soft laughter near the window. "No one will harm you because I will be with you always, and I will protect you from the evil things of this world. You are My precious daughter."

The love of the Lord in my life was more real than it had ever been. I knew He loved me. In light of such an amazing reality, how could I ever be afraid?

The experience of that evening taught me I never again needed to fear Satan, evil, or myself, because the Lord had promised that He would be with me forever.

Day 10

COMING INTO THE KINGDOM

Now this I say, brethren, that flesh and blood cannot inherit the kingdom of God; nor does corruption inherit incorruption.

—1 CORINTHIANS 15:50

Perhaps you can imagine how surprised I was. He had transported me from my bed and had given me a new body that enabled me to fly and walk with Him. The Lord of heaven and earth had suspended the laws of gravity, time, and space to show me things I will never forget.

The joy was so intense I felt as if I could touch it. I knew I had been transported to a different world. But where was it? Why was this happening? What did it mean?

The Lord answered my questions clearly and emphatically. "My daughter, we went to the kingdom."

Dear Father, may all my "kingdom experiences" encourage in my heart an ever-deepening longing for You, even as my will to serve You grows more all-encompassing as well...

Day 11

THE POND AND THE

Then David danced before the L
might.

—2 SAMUEL 6:14

Most assuredly, I say to you, unless one is born of water and the Spirit, he cannot enter the kingdom of God.

—JOHN 3:5

Dear Jesus, may the water of life wash over me each day, and may my dance of joy reflect the desire of my heart to be in never-ending fellowship with You…

In the center of this glorious place was a pond. A variety of fruit trees grew close to the rock wall, ringed by a magnificent profusion of lovely flowers. Scattered throughout were huge, gray boulders that seemed to be strategically placed for sitting and resting.

The pond really intrigued me; as soon as I saw it I began to sing in the Spirit and dance for joy. I can't really explain why I reacted that way, but something supernatural propelled me to express my gratitude, happiness, and peace in a demonstrable way.

The pond reminded me of a verse in the Book of Revelation: "And the Spirit and the bride say, 'Come!' And let him who hears say, 'Come!' And let him who thirsts come. And whoever desires, let him take the water of life freely" (Rev. 22:17).

THE LABORERS ARE FEW

But as many as received Him, to them He gave the right to become children of God, even to those who believe in His name: who were born, not of blood, nor of the will of the flesh, nor of the will of man, but of God.

—JOHN 1:12–13

Now I knew that He would simply speak through me and reach out to others. I only had to be willing to be used by Him.

Jesus went on, "Many people think I will never come for them, but I tell you, I am coming sooner than they realize."

When He said this the tone of His voice changed. I sensed a great urgency in His words. It was a warning, a message I had to share—and share now. The End Times are truly upon us. Jesus is coming soon.

"We have a lot of work to do."

O Jesus, let my thoughts be those that only You inspire, my voice the voice of compassion and caring, my words the words of love given by Your Holy Spirit . . .

Day 13

THE BLOOD OF ATONEMENT

He came to His own, and His own did not receive Him.

—JOHN 1:11

Because you have kept My command to persevere, I also will keep you from the hour of trial which shall come upon the whole world, to test those who dwell on the earth. Behold, I come quickly! Hold fast what you have, that no one may take your crown.

—REVELATION 3:10–11

Dear Jesus, I pray that my commitment to live as You direct might be as strong as my trust in the power of Your shed blood...

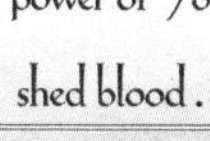

As the waves ebbed and flowed in front of us an amazing thing happened. The edge of the water turned to blood. A dark red, foaming, filthy-looking surf surged in front of us.

"Why is the blood so dirty?"

"It is My blood," He said. "It has washed away all the sins of My children."

I began to weep. He had shed His blood for me, to cleanse me of all my sins. He who knew no sin became sin for me, so I could be clothed with the righteousness of God.

"Even so," He said, "some of My children do not believe, and even some who believe do not live by My words."

Day 14

TOTALLY TRUSTING

Trust in the LORD with all your heart, and lean not on your own understanding; in all your ways acknowledge Him, and He shall direct your paths.

—PROVERBS 3:5–6

I sensed that the Lord was calling me to depend totally on Him—not on myself or anyone else but Him.

I determined that I would claim this promise from that moment on. I knew that the Lord would direct my path each step of the way. I also knew the truth of His promise: "Your word is a lamp to my feet and a light to my path" (Ps. 119:105). I committed myself to walking in the light of God's Word from then on.

I believed that Jesus would always be with me. Therefore, I would never need to fear again. He had spoken to me. He had held my hand. He had comforted me. He had made promises to me.

How could I ever doubt His presence, His reality, His truth?

My Savior, I ask that the faith You give me so abundantly might be strengthened into trust, that it might overshadow doubt and turn belief into certain knowledge of Your daily provision . . .

Day 15

Lord, I pray not for material abundance but for the wisdom to see the grace You have already poured out upon me, to bring myself into constant harmony with Your perfect vision for my life . . .

Infinite Patience, Infinite Grace

Call to Me, and I will answer you, and show you great and mighty things, which you do not know.

—Jeremiah 33:3

Though I wavered from time to time, Jesus was always faithful. He patiently and lovingly reminded me of the power of His presence that I had experienced firsthand.

I was learning that if He told me to do something, then He would enable me to accomplish it. I never asked for the gifts He so lavishly and graciously poured out upon me, but I did remember praying for the gifts of healing and ministry that would enable me to lead others to Him.

Now He was answering those prayers in ways that far exceeded my expectations. That's the kind of God we serve.

Day 16

ONE OF THE WORST

Let the little children come to Me, and do not forbid them; for of such is the kingdom of God.

—MARK 10:14

"Why are there so many babies here?"

"These are babies of mothers who did not want them," the Lord answered.

I then understood that these babies had been aborted from their mothers' wombs, and I began to cry. The Lord does not like abortion. It is one of the worst of all sins to Him. Jesus loves little children, and I could see His tender compassion for these babies as I watched and listened to Him.

Since that time I have been praying for the women of our nation, asking God to open their eyes to the truth, to keep them from making the wrong choice. I now know that the choice of abortion has eternal consequences, and I pray that the numbing of the American conscience will cease.

I can still hear the Lord's angry voice trembling with emotion: "I do not like abortion!"

Dear Lord, in Your infinite mercy may You look down upon us and grant greater awareness of the tragedy upon us, that we might love our unborn even more than we love ourselves, even as You love them since their moment of creation...

Day 17

GIVING BACK THE ULTIMATE

I beseech you therefore, brethren, by the mercies of God, that you present your bodies a living sacrifice, holy, acceptable to God, which is your reasonable service. And do not be conformed to this world, but be transformed by the renewing of your mind, that you may prove what is that good and acceptable and perfect will of God.

—ROMANS 12:1–2

Dearest Jesus, may all my gifts of myself be acceptable in Your sight, whether great or small, offered without hesitation or reservation . . .

The next stop on our heavenly itinerary was the huge white mansion where Jesus had taken me before. Again, I noticed that inside the great room were many men but very few women.

"These are people who sacrificed for Me," He said.

I wondered how many of them were the patriarchs and saints of the Bible, and I remembered faith's "Hall of Fame" in Hebrews 11.

Abel's sacrifice was more excellent than Cain's because it was presented in faith and obedience. Abraham's willingness to sacrifice his own son to the Lord confirmed his faith and his desire to please the Lord. And now I knew that God honors such sacrifices. In fact, He calls us to surrender everything to Him.

My heart leaped within as I recommitted everything to my Lord and Master. This, I realized, was the sacrifice He required of me.

Day 18

MORE IN HEAVEN THAN EARTH

Heal the sick there, and say to them, "The kingdom of God has come near to you."

—LUKE 10:9

Then the Lord took me to the peaceful pond where we had spent such wonderful times of fellowship together. This time we just sat and talked.

"I am telling you all this and showing you these things so you can tell the world. A lot of My children don't think I will come back for them for a long time. Some even think I will never come back. But My kingdom is ready for those who are waiting for Me. I am coming very soon.

"In the meantime I will never leave you. I will guide everything you do. I am releasing My power to you and in you. You will be able to heal the sick and do the same things I did when I lived on earth. The key to these gifts is your faith."

From that day forward I have felt like I'm living more in heaven than on earth. Truly, I know that heaven is so real, and that makes all the difference in this world.

O Lord, even as the focus of my eyes must be on temporary things, may the focus of my heart be on the infinite, eternal things of Your kingdom awaiting me even now . . .

Day 19

THEY SHALL FLEE TO THE MOUNTAINS

For a fire is kindled in My anger, and shall burn to the lowest hell; it shall consume the earth with her increase, and set on fire the foundations of the mountains.

—DEUTERONOMY 32:22

Soon the beach around us filled with frightened people. The fire they were fleeing from now consumed the surrounding area. Outbursts of flame popped up from the ocean as from miniature volcanoes, and the flames began to creep toward the shoreline. I began to sob as I heard the screams of the mob around me.

"Why are You showing this to me, Lord?" I asked.

"All the things you see are going to happen very soon. So many people do not believe My Word, so I have chosen you to help them see the truth. What I show to you I want you to tell the world."

There was anger in the Lord's voice. We left the rock where we were sitting and walked along the sand.

Heavenly Father, might I learn to direct my own anger toward my own failures to worship You rather than to others, and may I remain focused on Your will for the way I spend my time . . .

Day 20

To Worship God Forever

Come up here, and I will show you things which must take place after this.

—Revelation 4:1

I had the privilege once again of standing before the Lord's throne with so many others. I joined in the worship, and it was a wonderful time of peace, adoration, joy, and blessing.

This is what we have been created for—to worship God and enjoy Him forever. This is how we will spend all eternity. The scene in front of me was exactly as described in the Book of Revelation, in which John writes:

> Immediately I was in the Spirit; and behold, a throne set in heaven, and One sat on the throne. And He who sat there was like a jasper and a sardius stone in appearance; and there was a rainbow around the throne, in appearance like an emerald.
>
> —Revelation 4:2–3

I knew from what the Lord had told me that people were not heeding the words of Revelation, and now He wanted me to reiterate its message so that as many as possible would truly believe.

Lord, I ask You for the words to put into expression the things You bring to my awareness and the courage to put into motion the actions You inspire me to take . . .

Day 21

TO PREPARE A PLACE

In My Father's house are many mansions; if it were not so, I would have told you. I go to prepare a place for you. And if I go and prepare a place for you, I will come again and receive you to Myself; that where I am, there you may be also. And where I go you know, and the way you know.

—JOHN 14:2–4

Dear Jesus, may the temporal life I m living now be part of my preparation for eternal life in Your glorious presence, and may my life be focused on You alone . . .

Jesus took my hand and led me out of the throne room into a big, beautiful flower garden. The peace of this immense place filled me with love. I began to sing with joy, and a smile came automatically to my face.

As I turned in another direction I noticed a beautiful river. Along the river was a rock wall, and magnificent dwellings were situated on the left side. Many of these looked like castles where only the very wealthy might live.

The Lord said, "These are houses for My special children."

Now I know those mansions and castles are real, and the Lord has already prepared them for us. He wants us to be with Him there forever!

O Lord, I pray that the impossibility of entering Your kingdom by our own means might help to focus the lives of Your faithful more fully on You, not to discourage or eliminate those who would serve, but to refine and renew…

NO EASY ENTRY

And again I say unto you, it is easier for a camel to go through the eye of a needle than for a rich man to enter into the kingdom of God.
—MATTHEW 19:24

"The only ones who will enter My kingdom are the pure of heart—My obedient children," He said. "Many who call themselves 'Christians' do not live by My Word. Some think that going to church once a week is enough. They never read My words, and they pursue worldly things. Some who even know My words never have their hearts with Me."

The whole plan and purpose of God was beginning to clarify in my thinking. I remembered how Jesus had warned us of how hard it is to enter His kingdom, and now I had an inkling of what that meant.

"My Word says that it is hard to enter the kingdom of heaven, but so few really believe this and understand its importance. I am revealing this to you so you can warn them."

Day 23

ONLY THROUGH HIS WORD

Upon the wicked He will rain coals; fire and brimstone and a burning wind shall be the portion of their cup.

—PSALM 11:6

Father, I ask for awareness on the part of all Your children, especially that we might recognize the danger of partial commitment. May our passion to serve You be fully developed and always activated...

We climbed over a narrow road lined with trees and bushes. We strolled along this lane, which wound around a mountain. Near the summit we rested on a huge rock shaped like a gigantic bear.

I looked toward the ocean and noticed that its water had turned to blood once more. Again I saw people running on the beach. These were not casual joggers; they were running in fear and panic.

The bloody ocean had turned into a cauldron of blazing brimstone. The sand was a bed of hot, flaming coals. The people were running from the fire that pursued them, surrounded them, and licked hungrily at their bodies. No place was safe.

I was screaming the whole time, and I began to sob. "When will this happen, Lord?"

"After I bring My children home. Many people do not believe My Word. I love all My children, but I cannot bring them to My kingdom if they are not ready for Me. I will never force My children to do anything if they don't have a heart for Me."

IN THE FLAMES

But the day of the Lord will come as a thief in the night, in which the heavens will pass away with a great noise, and the elements will melt with fervent heat; both the earth and the works that are in it will be burned up.

—2 PETER 3:10

There is no word that truly identifies what I felt at that moment. It was a mixture of fear, desperation, hurt, terror, sadness, and hopelessness.

"I am showing this to you, My daughter, so you will fully understand that, no matter how good people are, they will go to hell if they do not accept Me."

I nodded my head.

"I know it hurts you to see them, but you must include this experience in the book. You have to warn the people of the world about the reality of hell. I want to see as many souls saved as possible before I return to gather My church unto Myself."

Dearest Jesus, I ask that the future pain we will feel at the loss of our loved ones might become a present force, compelling us to speak to them of You, often and convincingly as You lead…

Heavenly Father, I pray that our love for You might serve as a model for the love and respect we extend with the animals You have created, that all might one day live in complete harmony within the bounty of Your kingdom...

TRUE HARMONY, TRUE PEACE

It shall come to pass that before they call, I will answer; and while they are still speaking, I will hear. The wolf and the lamb shall feed together, the lion shall eat straw like the ox, and dust shall be the serpent's food. They shall not hurt nor destroy in all My holy mountain, says the LORD.

—ISAIAH 65:24–25

After the horrifying vision of hell, the Lord and I descended the mountain, passed through the dark tunnel, and returned to a place I had started to call "animal mountain." This is a wonderful place—a place of peace and joy where all the animals coexist in delightful harmony.

After seeing the tormenting fires of hell, this scene was most reassuring. Heaven is a place of peace and joy in contrast with the violence and depression of hell. The Lord's "animal mountain" is a place of eternal happiness.

It is reassuring to know that animals will live with us in paradise. Heaven is a place of beautiful flowers and glorious radiance, where people and animals alike will never experience pain, hardship, death, or suffering again.

Day 26

TO SACRIFICE SO MUCH

By faith Abraham obeyed when he was called to go out to the place which he would afterward receive as an inheritance. And he went out, not knowing where he was going. By faith he dwelt in the land of promise as in a foreign country, dwelling in tents with Isaac and Jacob, the heirs with him of the same promise; for he waited for the city which has foundations, whose builder and maker is God.

—HEBREWS 11:8–10

We walked across a golden bridge toward the white building, where the Lord introduced me to a very impressive gentleman. "I want you to meet Abraham," He said.

Abraham! The great patriarch of faith and obedience who had defied the entire world by proclaiming there is only one God. He put his hand on my shoulder and simply said, "Daughter."

The smile on his face told me that his blessing was upon my life, and I immediately loved this great man to whom I, and every believer in the world, owe so much. Abraham, like God, had willingly offered his only son.

In the same way, our heavenly Father gave His only begotten Son—Jesus—as a sacrifice for our sins. He was crucified and buried, but on the third day God raised Jesus from the dead, and because of His resurrection none of us ever have to fear death again.

Dearest Jesus, I recognize that You were the ultimate sacrifice and that Abraham was a man of ultimate faith. May my own faith be equally strong, my own willingness to serve You be of equivalent strength wherever and however You may call me . . .

Day 27

OUTSIDE THE GATE... FOREVER

For we must all appear before the judgment seat of Christ, that each one may receive the things done in the body, according to what he has done, whether good or bad.

—2 CORINTHIANS 5:10

He took me to another high mountain from which I could look down into another endless valley, where a multitude of people were wandering about in dejection. They looked weak and lost, and their gray faces matched their gray robes. They stared at the ground, shuffling aimlessly and hopelessly.

"Who are these people, Lord?"

"They are the sinful 'Christians.'"

I wondered why these people were here, and then I remembered that their valley leads to the burning pit. These so-called "Christians," who don't really know the Lord and who continually and willfully sin, will be eternally lost.

Then it occurred to me. When the Lord took me to see the dreadful places, we would go on different roads that were outside the gate of the heavenly kingdom.

My Savior, I pray that we might all avoid the willful sin that comes from failure to take Your Word seriously, that we might trust You for the truth and act instantly upon it . . .

Day 28

ON THE BEACH

Then many false prophets will rise up and deceive many. And because lawlessness will abound, the love of many will grow cold. But he who endures to the end shall be saved.

—MATTHEW 24:11–13

Suddenly I noticed that the mountains where the fires had burned the day before were now only charred mounds of ash and rubble. The ocean, once filled with blazing blood, was now a large, empty sinkhole.

God had shown me the very things He had already described in Revelation 8:8: "And something like a great mountain burning with fire was thrown into the sea, and a third of the sea became blood."

"When will all this take place?"

"After I bring My children to My kingdom. Whoever has read My book and believes My prophets should know about these things. All the things I showed you on this beach will happen very soon."

Jesus' words are real, and His prophecies will soon come to pass.

Our Father, may the Holy Spirit quicken our senses and help us realize the urgency of the times, that none of us might dally too long in our unbelief . . .

Day 29

JUST OVER THE HILLTOP

In my Father's house are many mansions: if it were not so, I would have told you. I go to prepare a place for you.

—JOHN 14:2

Heavenly Father, I pray that I might reach always for You and Your blessings, that I might trust Your Word rather than the fleeting pleasures of earth...

We walked past many mansions and castles, each more exquisite than the last. In front of one of these dwellings the Lord stopped. My heart kept skipping beats as we walked up the front steps.

This was the place Jesus had prepared for me. Here I was, standing at the door of a regal palace in heaven, with my name inscribed in gold on its beautiful door! It was too much to take in. How could these things be?

I cried tears of gratitude and joy, and my heart overflowed with love and adoration for the Lord. I had never anticipated such wonderful things. I had always felt that if He simply noticed me it would be OK.

I had tasted the living water, and I knew I would never thirst again. I had tasted the purple fruit of paradise, and I could never hunger for things of the world again.

Day 30

DAYS OF PREPARATION

God is my strength and power, and He makes my way perfect.

—2 SAMUEL 22:33

The strength of the Lord's anointing kept me from eating very much for periods of several days at a time. The sleep deprivation and lack of food caused me to feel weak and emaciated. Before leaving each day, however, the Lord would heal me of any pain.

We must remember—Jesus wept. He knew the pain of loneliness and rejection. He faced temptation. He wrestled with the will of God. He experienced anger and fear. No matter what we face, He has been there.

He also knew that many things had to be healed in my inner life before I could be effectively used. I was being prepared for a ministry of evangelism and healing that would begin with *Heaven Is So Real!*

Dear Lord, help me to bear up under the physical burdens of this world, not for worldly purposes but that I might do the work You have assigned me and provide the example You expect, not only of me but of all who would serve You . . .

JOURNAL

If Jesus appeared before me today, I would…

JOURNAL

PART II

A PREPARED PLACE FOR GOD'S CHILDREN

Day 31

Dearest Jesus, I thank You for the men and women You have raised up through the centuries to do Your work, for their willingness to serve, for their faithfulness, for the examples of their lives of service to You…

WRITERS OF THE WORD

For now we see in a mirror, dimly, but then face to face. Now I know in part, but then I shall know just as I also am known.

—1 CORINTHIANS 13:12

Several men were in front of us. "These are the ones who wrote My Word," the Lord said.

I looked at each glowing face and tried to guess who each one was. John, Matthew, Luke, Mark, James, Peter, Paul. The prophets were there as well—men such as Isaiah, Jeremiah, Micah, Malachi, Daniel, Hosea, and many others.

I thought, *Moses and Joshua must be in the crowd as well, and Nehemiah, Job, David, Solomon, and Jonah.* I wished I had time to talk with each one. I'd ask Jonah what it was like to be in the belly of the great fish. I'd want Daniel to tell me how it felt to be in the lion's den. I'd love to hear David describe his experience with Goliath.

Then it dawned on me. One day in the near future, I will take up my heavenly abode and have lasting fellowship with the saints of all ages! Then I will ask them. Then I will know.

Won't it be wonderful?

Made New Again

And God shall wipe away all tears from their eyes; and there shall be no more death, neither sorrow, nor crying, neither shall there be any more pain: for the former things are passed away.

—Revelation 21:4

An angel escorted me back to the changing room, where I could see my reflection in the huge, clear mirrors. I had been transformed! My new body was that of my teenage years. I was young, beautiful, and vibrant. Each time I saw the transformation I was shocked.

But it was a reminder that when we get to heaven we will have new bodies.

Our heavenly bodies will not grow old, and they will know no pain. There will be no wrinkles in our faces. Our teeth will be white and even. No gray will be found in our hair. The radiance of youth will glow from our eyes. Our posture will be straight. Any handicaps we experienced on earth will vanish.

We will be completely new in every respect!

O Lord, even as I behold this earthly vessel I look beyond it to the beauty, the radiance, the limitless capabilities of the heavenly body You have prepared for me, and I thank You for this gift . . .

Day 33

Father, even as a tiny bit of fear might help to move us forward, may we welcome every difficult circumstance, every gentle pruning, every casting into the fires of preparation that temper us and build us up for Your service . . .

A LITTLE BIT OF FEAR

Do not be wise in your own eyes; fear the LORD *and depart from evil.*

—PROVERBS 3:7

He seemed focused on helping me gain confidence, first in Him and then in myself.

"My daughter, I have shown you the important parts of the kingdom of God, and I want you to tell everyone what you have seen. When you do the work I have called you to do, many souls will be saved. The book will be read all over the world."

"But, Lord, I am nobody. Why did You choose me? Why not someone who is famous already?"

"I created you for this End-Time work. I know you are learning what I teach you. I know you will be faithful to Me."

My problem was not in trusting the Lord. My problem was in trusting myself. Since my childhood I had always been afraid to step out, to take the lead—and now I was being called to write a book and launch a ministry.

Actually, I was frightened.

IN HIS STRENGTH AND POWER

I can do all things through Christ who strengthens me.

—PHILIPPIANS 4:13

He then said something that was vitally important to Him, "Before I come for My people, half of the unbelievers will be saved."

Isn't it thrilling to know that half of the unbelievers in the world will be saved before the Lord returns? Many millions of people will be ushered into the church of Jesus Christ, and the church had better be prepared.

I was learning that God enables those He calls. He fills in the empty places and provides strength in our weakness. Like the handicapped people I'd seen in the vision of the church, without Him we're all limited in one way or another.

But God is able to give new strength to the legs of the lame, and as He heals our handicaps we are able to walk in newness of life—in the strength and power of His Holy Spirit.

Dear Jesus, I cast upon Your mercies every handicap I might ever have, every infirmity, every limitation both physical and mental, for Your gracious healing in Your own perfect time . . .

Day 35

Green Pastures

The LORD *is my shepherd; I shall not want. He makes me to lie down in green pastures; He leads me beside the still waters. He restores my soul.*

—PSALM 23:1–3

Dear Father, as I walk through the valley may my heart be on the mountain-top; as the shadow of death passes before me may I see only eternal life at Your side…

I imagined what it must have been like for the original disciples who had to say good-bye to their Lord and Master. How must His mother, Mary, have felt when she saw Him crucified, dead, and buried? How did she feel when He ascended into heaven?

By this time every waking moment of my life was filled with thoughts of Jesus and heaven. I had been in the Lord's company daily for more than one and a half months. I had been to heaven and had seen the streets of gold, the mansions over the hilltop, the River of Life.

I had been escorted by angels and had fellowshiped and worshiped with the saints, martyrs, apostles, and prophets. I had walked into the eternal dwelling Jesus had already prepared for me. I knew I could never be the same again. Nothing in this world could compare.

Then it occurred to me that the rest He was wanting me to take was part of the preparation He was doing in my life. The Lord, my Shepherd, was permitting me to lie down in the green pastures so my soul could be restored.

Day 36

THE CALL TO REST

There remains therefore a rest for the people of God. For he who has entered His rest has himself also ceased from his works as God did from His. Let us therefore be diligent to enter that rest, lest anyone fall after the same example of disobedience.

—HEBREWS 4:9–11

O Jesus, thank You for the rest that I find in You; thank You for the joy I find in Your service; thank You for the love and mercy and patience that overwhelm me daily . . .

Soon my whole body began to shake. I groaned in the spirit for more than fifteen minutes. Then, as had happened so many times before, the Lord appeared, sitting by the window next to the bed.

"My precious daughter, I told you I will be with you always. You are going to see Me anytime you want, and you will hear My voice."

"Lord," I said, "I want to do everything You tell me. I still feel I do not know anything."

"That is precisely why I chose you. Never forget that I will take care of you. I have given you this special gift because no one knows you. Soon, however, everyone will know you."

I found it hard to accept those words. But the Lord, in His mercy and patience, saw fit to visit me again to give me this reassuring message. "I want you to rest," He said, and then He left.

The Lord wanted me to rest because He was preparing me for ministry. Yet knowing that He was coming back to escort me to heaven again brought such peace to my soul.

Lord, may the cares of this world disappear; the worries of today give way to a bright tomorrow; the fears and timidity that constrain me give way to clarity, boldness, and unshakable trust in Your provision . . .

THE ULTIMATE FOCUS

But seek first the kingdom of God and His righteousness, and all these things shall be added to you. Therefore do not worry about tomorrow, for tomorrow will worry about its own things.

—MATTHEW 6:33–34

The power He was unleashing in my body was beginning to heal the weak places in my character that remained from my childhood. I was learning how to be more confident, how to reach out and truly trust the Lord.

Even so, I still struggled with certain worries and fears, so I was not surprised when He said to me: "I see that you are pure-hearted. I've seen your obedience, and I know you fear My words. From here on I want you to concentrate only on My work and nothing else."

As we walked back down from the mountain, on the sand, I felt incredibly happy—as if a great burden had been lifted. Truly the Lord had shown me many new things that brought healing and freedom to my timid soul. I felt like a new person.

Day 38

FAITH OR WORRY; NEVER BOTH

Whatever is not from faith is sin.

—ROMANS 14:23

I began to delve into the Scriptures to see what I could learn about the sin of worry. My eyes were drawn to these words of Jesus: "But seek first the kingdom of God and His righteousness, and all these things shall be added to you. Therefore do not worry about tomorrow, for tomorrow will worry about its own things" (Matt. 6:33–34).

The context of this passage is the Sermon on the Mount, in which Jesus shares the secrets of spiritual victory with His disciples. Like me, the disciples were fretting over so many things. They worried if they would have food to eat and clothing to wear.

Jesus reminded them:

> So why do you worry about clothing? Consider the lilies of the field, how they grow: they neither toil nor spin; and yet I say to you that even Solomon in all his glory was not arrayed like one of these. Now if God so clothes the grass of the field, which today is, and tomorrow is thrown into the oven, will He not much more clothe you, O you of little faith?
>
> —MATTHEW 6:28–30

That's the key—faith! That's why worry is a sin—it is not of faith. God wants us to walk by faith. Why should we ever worry again?

My Savior, I ask not only that my sins be forgiven, but that my inability to trust in You at every moment be overcome by faith so strong it can never let doubt creep back into my consciousness . . .

Day 39

Heavenly Father, I ask that You might send the Holy Spirit to help me pray, not so that all my prayers might be answered but that I might pray in ways that please You, in words that bless You, in thoughts that touch Your heart as You touch mine…

FOR PRAYERS TO BE HEARD…

The LORD is far from the wicked, but He hears the prayers of the righteous.

—PROVERBS 15:29

As He sat on the rock on the mountainside, Jesus said, "Don't concern yourself with testifying in church. Concentrate on My work.

"I want you to write about how you live your Christian life. It is important for others to know how you have lived your life with Me, to see how open your heart has been to Me. I know you always put Me first in your life—that I'm more important to you than anyone or anything else in the world.

"I want you to know that I've heard all your prayers even though it may seem that I have not answered each one. I know the hearts of all My children. I cannot bless anyone who does not have a sincere heart, but I do want all My children to be blessed."

After He left me this time I reflected on His words. He had seemed so genuinely pleased with me, and I was thrilled to know that He had heard all my prayers. God truly does hear and answer the sincere prayers of His children.

Day 40

NO POSSIBLE COMPARISON

However, Jesus did not permit him, but said to him, "Go home to your friends, and tell them what great things the Lord has done for you, and how He has had compassion on you."

—MARK 5:19

Dearest Jesus, may my heart be as pure as the message of Your Word, and may my thoughts be forever focused on the things of God, not the things of this world . . .

The Lord began to speak.

"When I was on this earth I knew what I would have to face, but I lived for My Father's words. That's why all of heaven and earth are Mine now.

"So many of My children know what I want them to do, but they still love the things of this world more. The children who live according to My Word are the ones who are pure of heart.

"They are the only ones who will enter the mansions I've prepared for them. No one can have both this kingdom and My kingdom as well."

I'll never forget those words—and I know they are so true. This life has nothing to compare with the kingdom of God. I've seen it, and I know His kingdom is prepared for us.

WOUNDS OF ENDLESS LOVE

But He was wounded for our transgressions, He was bruised for our iniquities; the chastisement for our peace was upon Him, and by His stripes we are healed.

—ISAIAH 53:5

As I thought of the Lord's suffering and read scriptures related to His passion, I began to cry. At that moment I saw Jesus in front of me. "My daughter, I want you to look at My hands again." He pointed to the scars on His hands and feet. I sat in the Lord's presence in total silence as He continued to speak.

"I want you to keep on writing everything I show you."

I nodded. Throughout the remainder of the service I cried under the precious anointing of the Holy Spirit. The shaking subsided when the Lord left, but the tears did not.

I heard the pastor's words, but my mind and spirit were focused on something else…

Dear Father, I pray that I might never forget the suffering You endured for me, not to focus on the pain but to remember the joy of salvation You brought about for all who will open their hearts and accept it…

Day 42

AT THE CROSS

And when they had come to a place called Golgotha, that is to say, Place of a Skull, they gave Him sour wine mingled with gall to drink. But when He had tasted it, He would not drink. Then they crucified Him, and divided His garments, casting lots.

—MATTHEW 27:33–35

I could see my precious Lord and Master hanging on the cross. The sharp spikes ripped at the flesh of His palms and ankles. The Roman soldier's spear opened a gaping wound in His side, and streams of blood coursed down His face from the crown of thorns.

A puddle of blood lay at the foot of the cross, in which the people stepped as they clambered after His seamless robe. They mocked Him, spit at Him, and cursed Him.

Then I saw His mother—Mary—bowing near the cross, her body trembling and tears forming rivers on her face. Oh, how I understood how she must have felt.

Jesus could have called ten thousand angels, but instead He accepted the cruel, shameful death of crucifixion so we could find the path of life. The scars on His hands and feet are the marks of horrendous suffering—anguish He experienced for you and me.

Dear Jesus, may the price You paid for my salvation move me to witness to others, that they may see the same immortal truths and know the same eternal joy . . .

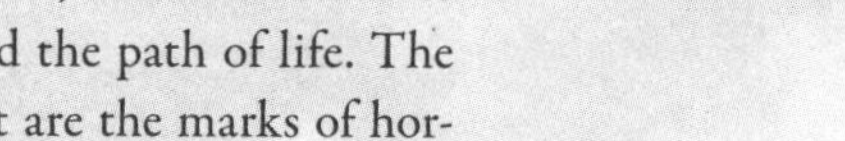

Day 43

THE NEW JERUSALEM

Behold, I am coming quickly! Hold fast what you have, that no one may take your crown. He who overcomes, I will make him a pillar in the temple of My God, and he shall go out no more. I will write on him the name of My God and the name of the city of My God, the New Jerusalem, which comes down out of heaven from My God. And I will write on him My new name.

—Revelation 3:11–12

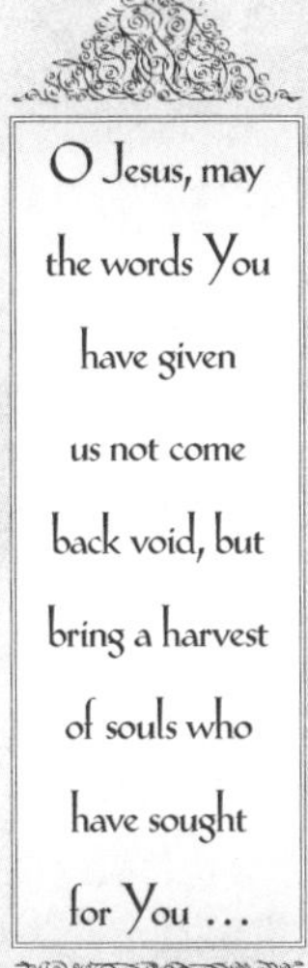

The minute we arrived at the pond again I began to sing and dance. My heart was still flying with joy. Then the Lord said, "My daughter, I showed you the river and New Jerusalem. Those houses are in Jerusalem—the Holy City. We will all live there when I bring My children home.

"I know some people will not believe many of the things I've shown you—the doubtful and the ones who don't know My Word—but I know how hard you are trying to please Me.

"You will be a surprise to all the churches, a joy to those ready and waiting for Me and sad news to those who love the world more than Me."

Day 44

NO LOSS; ONLY GAIN

And he carried me away in the Spirit to a great and high mountain, and showed me the great city, the holy Jerusalem, descending out of heaven from God, having the glory of God. And her light was like a most precious stone, like a jasper stone, clear as crystal.

—REVELATION 21:10–11

Dear Lord, I pray that my commitment to You will never waver; may it be as strong years from now as it is today . . .

One thing I know for sure—since I became a Christian I have always endeavored to please my Lord, to put Him first in every situation and every decision. He was blessing my obedience.

"It took a long time to prepare you for this work," He said. "Now you know how special you are to Me. You said that you had given your life to Me, and I know your heart. Don't ever deviate from this commitment.

"Whatever you have to lose in your earthly life will be restored to you in heaven. And you will be with Me there."

To me, those were the most important words of all. This promise kept me going, for knowing that I would be in His presence forever was the most blessed thought of all.

Day 45

In the Body or Out

I know a man in Christ who fourteen years ago—whether in the body I do not know, or whether out of the body I do not know... was caught up to the third heaven. And I know such a man... how he was caught up into Paradise and heard inexpressible words, which it is not lawful for a man to utter.

—2 Corinthians 12:2–4

Father, I pray that my dedication to You might be increased daily, that my faith might be built into a mighty edifice of trust, that my heart might always belong entirely to You in all possible ways...

I began to think of the individuals in the Bible with whom I shared the privilege of visiting heaven before death. I know exactly what the apostle Paul experienced, for there are many things I saw and heard that I am not permitted to share.

The apostle John, as recorded in the Book of Revelation, also went to heaven. His visit was preceded by a personal visit from the Lord. Like John's, my visits to heaven always began with a visit from Him.

The prophet Elijah went to heaven as well. "Then it happened... that suddenly a chariot of fire appeared with horses of fire, and... Elijah went up by a whirlwind into heaven" (2 Kings 2:11).

How privileged I am to be among those He has honored in this way. It's not because I'm special, but simply because I want only to obey and serve my Lord throughout eternity.

Day 46

A Taste of Heaven

So He commanded the multitude to sit down on the ground. And He took the seven loaves and the fish and gave thanks, broke them and gave them to His disciples; and the disciples gave to the multitude. So they all ate and were filled, and they took up seven large baskets full of the fragments that were left.

—Matthew 15:35–37

The Lord waded into the water and grabbed a large, flat, white fish, about the size of my two hands together. I enjoyed watching Him do this, and I found the scene very amusing.

Next, I walked with Him beyond the rocks, where I noticed many large cooking areas with silver-colored ovens built into the rocks. Atop the ovens were cooking grilles with oval-shaped plates and silver forks. The Lord simply pushed a button on the side of one oven and a fire began.

He then assumed the role of a cook, right in front of me. He grilled the fish until both sides were brown. He seemed to be so happy doing this.

When we finished eating He took my plate and fork and put them into a silver container. "I love you, My precious daughter," He said, in a voice filled with happiness. "Tell everyone that everything here will taste so much better than any earthly food. Did you like the fish?"

I nodded my appreciation. As we stood, the Lord embraced me and then departed.

Heavenly Father, may the joys of heaven be so real to me that all the trials of earth seem fleeting and insignificant, with my eyes always fixed on You...

ON THE WATER OF LIFE

Dearest Jesus, I thank You for Your incomparable provision for all Your children, to join with You in a heavenly paradise made wholly joyful by Your presence and Your preparations . . .

You will show me the path of life; in Your presence is fullness of joy; at Your right hand are pleasures forevermore.

—Psalm 16:11

A huge river appeared in front of us, and I noticed mountains on both sides of the water. The one on the right was extremely high. We walked very close to the river, where the soil was like gravel. Tiny pebbles clicked under our feet.

The river was filled with small boats. We climbed into one of them, and the Lord paddled with His hand. He took us a good way out. When I looked over the edge I saw a multitude of different-colored fish frolicking in the water.

I was amazed by the clear water; it was like the clearest crystal I'd ever seen. The fish were amazingly bright and beautiful. They looked like the large decorative fish that people on earth put in their backyard ponds.

"These, My daughter, are for pleasure. Like you, I love to watch the fish swim around in the water."

It was so peaceful and serene on the quiet water. I felt as if we were sitting atop a giant looking glass.

Wings of Peace

When He had been baptized, Jesus came up immediately from the water; and behold, the heavens were opened to Him, and He saw the Spirit of God descending like a dove and alighting upon Him. And suddenly a voice came from heaven, saying, "This is My beloved Son, in whom I am well pleased."

—Matthew 3:16–17

For many centuries, the dove has symbolized two things: peace and the Holy Spirit. A dove announced to Noah that the waters of the Great Deluge had dried up. It's not surprising, therefore, that I encountered doves on my next visit to heaven.

We walked for a long while and then took a road to the right. We walked for quite a while on this road as well. It encircled the base of a large, rocky mountain. To our left was a wide valley, filled with green trees. The middle of the valley seemed to be filled with white gravel.

As I looked over the serene valley, I noticed movement in the region of the white gravel. The area was filled with birds.

"Lord, what kind of birds are those?"

"They are doves."

It was a magnificent place—so large and so beautiful. We climbed atop a solid rock wall upon which we could stand and watch the doves of heaven. We remained there for a long time, and I was profoundly moved by what I was seeing.

O Jesus, may the realities of Your salvation and the joys of my home in heaven inspire me to live each day on earth by focusing always on You and our shared eternity together . . .

Day 49

O Lord, I pray that I might always be "spiritually minded," that I might never entertain thoughts that detract from the reality of my salvation and the promise of eternity that You so graciously provide…

AT THE FEET OF THE MASTER

"My thoughts are not your thoughts, nor are your ways My ways," says the LORD. *"For as the heavens are higher than the earth, so are My ways higher than your ways, and My thoughts than your thoughts."*

—ISAIAH 55:8–9

After the visit to the heavenly sea, we went to the secluded pond where we often sat and talked. I loved these times of sweet communion with the Lord. I felt very much like Mary, who willingly sat at the Lord's feet to learn His ways.

Yes, I determined I would be like Mary. I chose the "good part" that will never be taken away from me, which is a personal relationship with Jesus Christ. Nothing in all the world is more important than that!

I wanted to have my mind renewed so I could see all things from a heavenly perspective.

I determined to take the heavenly perspective back to earth with me, to continue building on my relationship with the Lord, and to let Him continually renew my mind.

Day 50

OF ENDLESS WORSHIP

All nations whom You have made shall come and worship before You, O Lord, and shall glorify your name. For You are great, and do wondrous things; you alone are God.

—PSALM 86:9–10

Just as quickly as it had darkened, the room was filled with the most radiant light I had ever seen. I was stunned by its brightness and beauty.

I noticed steps leading to a platform where the Lord was sitting. He was dressed in pure gold. His golden crown glistened in the light, and His golden robe sparkled and shone.

Then the room filled with people who wore white gowns and silver crowns, bowing in the Lord's presence. It seemed as if the room began to expand to accommodate the rising number of people of all colors and types.

Then the Lord came toward me, wearing His regular white gown. "They worship Me continually," the Lord said, explaining why the people were there.

"May I worship You with them when I come back to heaven to be with You forever?" I asked.

The Lord chuckled and said, "Of course, My daughter. The place I showed you is where all My people will gather to worship Me."

Yes, heaven is so real!

Dear Father, grant that my worship of You might be pure of heart and unrestrained by the cares of distractions of this world, even as it serves as a mere shadow of the endless worship to come . . .

Day 51

IN THOSE DAYS

"I will be to Him a Father, and He shall be to Me a Son. . . . Let all the angels of God worship Him." And of the angels He says: "Who makes His angels spirits and His ministers a flame of fire."

—HEBREWS 1:5–7

Dear Jesus, no matter what my temptations might be, I pray that I might use these days not as though they were the end of an age, but as the beginning of limitless opportunities to serve You . . .

My experiences with Jesus and the heavenly home that all true believers will one day enjoy opened my eyes to several spiritual truths. I began to realize that in the same way God had created us in His own image, He had created earth in the image of heaven.

But in Satan's pride and envy he tempted the first people to disobey God. He lost his right to eternal glory in heaven because of his sin. In a similar way, Adam and Eve were banned from their earthly paradise, and those who do not obey God in this life will be banned from the heavenly paradise.

Many people, like me, are having intriguing experiences with angels in these last days. Angels are visiting us even as they did in ancient times. They are assuring people of the love of God, and they are warning them of things that are soon to come.

As Jesus has told me so often, we truly are in the last days.

Day 52

To Know That You Know

Rejoice and be exceeding glad, for great is your reward in heaven.

—Matthew 5:12

I will never again be as I was when I yearned to enjoy this earth for as many years as possible—to live to a ripe old age and travel here and there. I just want to be with the Lord. I know heaven is so real, and I know Jesus is always there. I love Him more than my life, and I want everyone to believe in Him, to know there is a heaven already prepared for them.

I used to wonder about these things, and sometimes I struggled to believe, but now I know that I know that I know. There is a heaven, and it is our true home.

I also knew that I didn't know much about writing books, and I knew very little about God's Word, except for the importance of being obedient and fearing the Lord. But He told me not to worry. I am finally learning how to surrender all my worries to Him, because I know He cares about me.

I want to do my best to please the Lord at all times.

Heavenly Father, I thank You for the knowledge and assurance You give so freely, that I can know for certain the power of Your love and the glory of Your provision, even for me . . .

Day 53

O Lord, might I abide in You as You abide in me, that Your grace and Your love might lift me up high as a lighthouse beacon, to reflect Your presence into the world around me . . .

ABIDE IN ME

If you abide in Me, and My words abide in you, you will ask what you desire, and it shall be done for you. By this My Father is glorified, that you bear much fruit; so you will be My disciples. As the Father loved Me, I also have loved you; abide in My love.

—John 15:7–9

"I know all your needs before you ask Me, but I never want My children to stop asking," the Lord said.

His words reminded me of something I had read in the Bible that very morning: "And when you pray, do not use vain repetitions as the heathen do. For they think that they will be heard for their many words. Therefore do not be like them. For your Father knows the things you have need of before you ask Him" (Matt. 6:7–8).

On this particular spring morning the Master was reminding me of these precious truths.

Day 54

AS A LITTLE CHILD

Assuredly, I say to you, whoever does not receive the kingdom of God as a little child will by no means enter it.

—MARK 10:15

The Lord wants us to become like little children so we can enjoy the blessings of the kingdom of heaven forever. Purity of heart, fascination, a sense of wonder, joy, present-moment living—all these are among the magical qualities of childhood that God wants us to exhibit to get to heaven.

However, because so many things come against us while we grow up, we quickly lose our innocence and our ability to trust. These are restored to us when we come, fully surrendered, to the Lord. It is a beautiful transformation: "Therefore, if anyone is in Christ, he is a new creation; old things have passed away; behold, all things have become new" (2 Cor. 5:17).

Jesus made it very clear to me that this is what He wants each of us to be like—to have the faith of a little child. Those who do not will never truly enter the joy of the Lord.

Father, I ask that my own faith might always be as simple and childlike as You Yourself have commanded, that I might never lose the sense of wonder I still associate with my first experience of You...

Day 55

OF THE PUREST HEART

For the Lord Himself will descend from heaven with a shout, with voice of an archangel, and with the trumpet of God. And the dead in Christ will rise first. Then we who are alive and remain shall be caught up together with them in the clouds to meet the Lord in the air.

—1 THESSALONIANS 4:16–17

Dearest Jesus, I pray that my own heart might be pure and true in every respect, that it might also wholly reflect the perfect safety and perfect love of Your presence . . .

Something miraculous will be happening in the very near future. The apostle Paul describes a cataclysmic event in which the Lord Jesus will return from heaven with His saints to "rapture" His church. It will be the ultimate experience for all who know Jesus.

But those who don't know the Lord will appear before the judgment seat of Christ, where they will hear the sentence that their lack of faith deserves— "for the wages of sin is death" (Rom. 6:23). Those who know Jesus, however, will receive the reward God has promised—"the gift of God is eternal life in Christ Jesus our Lord" (Rom. 6:23).

"I am ready for My children," the Lord said, "but so many of My children do not really believe and they are living for worldly things. I love all of them and want to bring all of them to heaven with Me, but I cannot take those who are not ready for Me.

"Those who come to My kingdom must be pure of heart and obedient."

THE ROCK OF MY REFUGE

The name of the LORD is a strong tower; the righteous run to it and are safe.

—PROVERBS 18:10

O Lord, may I always have the presence of mind and purity of heart to trust in You completely; may You always be my first resource and my only refuge . . .

God is love, and heaven is a place where love is the environment—it is the light and life of eternity with Him.

The vacuum in my own heart was filled by the tremendous love of God. After I gave my heart to Jesus I felt very secure, and it was easy for me to trust His love. I knew the truth of the hymn, "No One Ever Cared for Me Like Jesus."

Jesus had brought good news to me. He had healed my broken heart. He had set me free from my fears, my negative self-image, my insecurities. He had opened the eyes of my spirit and lifted my oppression.

I feel secure in the love of Jesus. He is my safe place, my high tower, my Rock of refuge. He will never let me down or leave me.

No Worry in Him

Come to Me, all you who labor and are heavy laden, and I will give you rest. Take my yoke upon you and learn from Me, for I am gentle and lowly in heart, and you will find rest for your souls. For My yoke is easy and My burden is light.

—Matthew 11:28–30

Father, may all my worries flee like the night before Your day, and all my doubts disappear like chaff before the winds of healing from Your throne . . .

Throughout my life, as I've mentioned several times, I've been prone to worry. It probably stems from the turmoil I experienced during my childhood. Whatever the reason, however, I often struggled with worry and fear and insecurity.

I knew this was not God's will for me, so I began to look at my worrying somewhat differently, calling it concern instead of worry. Somehow, saying that I was "concerned" rather than "worried" made it seem OK.

But the Lord has made it plain to me that He wants us to be totally honest with Him and with others as well as with ourselves. We cannot use the world's methods to justify, rationalize, or cover our sins. I knew that worry was a sin, and I had tried to pretend it was not there.

Why should we choose to worry when our Father promises us so much?

Day 58

IS YOUR NAME THERE?

If you confess with your mouth the Lord Jesus and believe in your heart that God has raised Him from the dead, you will be saved. For with the heart one believes unto righteousness, and with the mouth confession is made to salvation. For the Scripture says, "Whoever believes on Him will not be put to shame."

—ROMANS 10:8–11

Dear Jesus, I pray that my own choice might never be in doubt. I choose You! And I choose heaven! And I choose eternity in Your beloved presence . . .

Heaven is a choice. The Lord does not want anyone to end up in the pit of hell. If you believe, you will have eternal life with the Lord.

Indeed, the Book of Revelation describes two types of people. John speaks of the eternal destiny of the first, unfortunate group as follows: "And the smoke of their torment ascends forever and ever; and they have no rest day or night" (Rev. 14:11).

The second group, on the other hand, is described this way: "Here is the patience of the saints; here are those who keep the commandments of God and the faith of Jesus. . . . Blessed are the dead who die in the Lord from now on . . . that they may rest from their labors, and their works follow them" (Rev. 14:12–13).

Is your name written in the Lamb's Book of Life?

Day 59

THE HARDEST WORK

I have glorified You on the earth. I have finished the work which You have given Me to do. And now, O Father, glorify Me together with Yourself, with the glory which I had with You before the world was.

—JOHN 17:4–5

When I saw His crucified body there was blood streaming down His face and on His body. The crown of thorns was upon His head. His skin was tan, and His hair was dark and curly. His muscular body glistened with sweat.

The Lord's eyes were vividly penetrating and alive. He stood before me with His hands stretched out in the form of a cross.

It was the most amazing spiritual experience I had ever had. I felt breathless, and I cried throughout it. But the joy I experienced was so full that I felt I wanted to die for Him right at that moment.

When this vision was over, the Lord said, "This was the hardest work of all."

Dear Jesus, may Your supreme sacrifice bring about the salvation and the healing You so fervently desire, and may I take my rightful place among the saved of earth...

Day 60

FINAL PREPARATIONS

And there were noises and thunderings and lightnings; and there was a great earthquake, such a mighty and great earthquake as had not occurred since men were on the earth.

—REVELATION 16:18

I could see the whole world enveloped in a clear blue sky; then the scene changed to one with a heavy cloud cover. When the clouds began to break apart, fire rained down from the sky. The whole earth was ablaze, and then the fire changed to snow.

A second vision then came forth. This time the Lord showed me the whole world once more. The sky was filled with black clouds. Then it began to storm and rain. The lightning flashed, and many cities were destroyed. I could see the buildings within these cities collapsing.

I began to cry as the Lord told me that all of these things would begin to come to pass at that time.

Countless times He showed me similar visions and told me it is time to prepare for His coming.

Heavenly Father, I pray that we might all be prepared for Your coming, whether now or later, whether quietly or loudly; whether with blazing trumpets or a simple summons from Your righteous lips . . .

JOURNAL

Reflect on God's promises about heaven. What fresh revelations has He shared with you about this special place?

JOURNAL

Part III

Anointed for Ministry

Day 61

O Lord, may all my groanings be heard and understood by You; may the voice of my spirit speak to You through the office of Your Holy Spirit, sent to express things too wondrous and profound for me to say for myself . . .

HEART-TO-HEART

And He Himself gave some to be . . . prophets . . . for the equipping of the saints for the work of ministry, for the edifying of the body of Christ.

—Ephesians 4:11–12

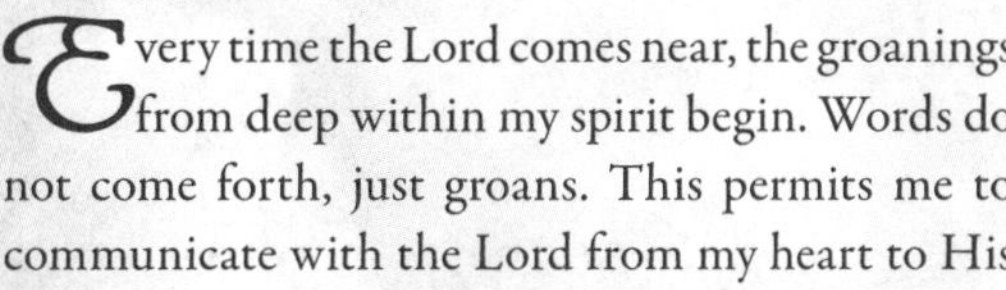

Every time the Lord comes near, the groanings from deep within my spirit begin. Words do not come forth, just groans. This permits me to communicate with the Lord from my heart to His heart, bypassing my voice and mind.

The Lord explained that heart-to-heart communication is the most important kind of fellowship. Satan is unable to hear what we are saying. During each session I would not be able to speak directly to the Lord with my voice, but only with my heart.

"My daughter, you are an End-Times prophetess," the Lord told me, "and you are living proof of My Word and My prophecies."

Now I realize that everything He shared with me is a confirmation of the words of His Bible, and the prophecies He gave me are echoes of His Word.

Day 62

ALL THE WORLD IS OURS

And you shall take the anointing oil, pour it on his head, and anoint him.

—EXODUS 29:7

The moon and stars brightened the sky, and I saw the Lord in a shaft of light as bright as the sun. He was wearing a gold crown and robe, and He was holding a golden ball that was covered with stones, which He was lowering from heaven. A bright and shiny brilliance surrounded Him.

My special vision-voice came forth, and I saw the Lord before me. He was holding the ball in both of His hands; then He put it in His right hand and said, "I will pour this anointing on your head."

When He removed the top of the ball, steam came out. After He poured it upon me He showed me the whole ocean and the world and said, "The world is yours."

Heavenly Father, my concern is for heaven, not the world; may this be the cry of my heart and the thought most often conveyed from my spirit to Yours...

Day 63

Dearest Jesus, may I never fail to remember the message You have given to all Your people, including me, that You are coming soon! May it be on my heart at all times and in my response when others ask me about You…

I HAVE CALLED YOU FRIENDS

You are My friends if you do whatever I command you. No longer do I call you servants, for a servant does not know what his master is doing; but I have called you friends, for all things that I heard from My Father I have made known to you.

—JOHN 15:14–15

I soon discovered that He knows everything about me. He often reminds me of my plans for a given day.

Even though He is my best friend, I am very humbled in His presence. I reverentially fear and respect Him very much, because I know He is God.

The urgency I feel for souls keeps me motivated at all times. Now I even want to help my enemies whenever I can. The Lord wants me to serve as living proof of the Bible and His prophecies, because many people do not believe what they read in the Bible.

Nor do they believe He is coming soon for His people.

WHOSE MIND IS STAYED ON THEE

But seek first the kingdom of God and His righteousness, and all these things shall be added to you.

—MATTHEW 6:33

Dear Jesus, may the infinite righteousness I see in You be reflected in my heart, my mind, and my spirit, that I might be righteous too not on my own, but through Your sacrifice and Your infinite love...

God even knows what we have need of before we express those needs to Him. I must admit that sometimes it's not easy to live a fully spiritual life, always putting God first. But I have learned that I cannot do anything without the Lord's permission.

He always tells me to stay focused on Him and the work He is preparing me for. It's been difficult, but I've learned that keeping my mind stayed on Him is the source of perfect peace.

If anything is bothering me I'm not able to focus on Him, and I lose my peace. I know this is not God's will for me, because Jesus said: "Peace I leave with you, My peace I give to you; not as the world gives do I give to you. Let not your heart be troubled, neither let it be afraid" (John 14:27).

The Lord is always a help in our lives, even when we can't see or hear Him. He is living in us, and that is how He knows everything about us.

Day 65

ULTIMATE REALITY

Blessed are the pure in heart, for they shall see God.

—MATTHEW 5:8

Our Father, I pray that the purity of my heart might not be the measure of myself but the reflection of You as Your Holy Spirit manifests Himself in me, not to my glory but to Yours...

At first everything was bright, and then I saw all of heaven. It was a place of purity and whiteness, and the roads and buildings were immaculately clean.

He took me into heaven once more and began to show me things, one by one. A brilliance like sunlight was everywhere.

Then the Lord showed me all the oceans of the world, with snow covering the whole earth. The Lord explained: "I must purify My people before I bring them to My kingdom. Unless they are pure-hearted, they cannot see My kingdom."

The Lord then repeated some of His previous lessons. He explained again that He wanted me to put them all down in the book. This helped me to better understand the title He gave to my book, *Heaven Is So Real!*

By repeating these lessons and experiences in my life, I began to realize exactly how real heaven is.

Day 66

ESSENCE OF WORSHIP

Rejoice always, pray without ceasing, in everything give thanks; for this is the will of God in Christ Jesus for you.

—1 THESSALONIANS 5:16–18

As the Master taught me more about prayer, I realized how very important it is in each of our lives. He told me to pray in tongues when I rise in the morning, until the flow ceases each Sunday before I go to church. Then He urged me to go to church thirty minutes early and to pray in tongues without interruption until the worship begins.

The people who understand why I do this have a deep, personal walk with the Lord. They understand what I mean when I say that Jesus is more real to me than I am to myself.

During all my prayer and worship times I give every ounce of my energy and attention to the Lord, for I believe that's what worship really is.

O Lord, I praise Your holy name and thank You for Your mercy toward me, that You in Your endless grace have looked upon me as one of Your children—saved, set apart, and made holy in Your sight . . .

Day 67

Father, may the mistakes of this life turn into the triumphs of eternal life that we might all learn the infinite truths You desire to teach us through our steps, our missteps, and our temporal failures . . .

THROUGH THE CHILDREN

Brethren, if a man is overtaken in any trespass, you who are spiritual restore such a one in a spirit of gentleness, considering yourself lest you also be tempted. Bear one another's burdens, and so fulfill the law of Christ.

—GALATIANS 6:1–2

The Lord taught us many things through our daughter. For a long while I was very ashamed of my daughter's divorce.

But I believe the Lord didn't like my shameful thoughts, and He gave me no choice but to include my daughter's story in my book. I never questioned Him about why I had to do this.

Now her life is settled, and our relationship is like it used to be. Better still, through that process I learned that the things that happen to our children may have nothing to do with their walk with God, or with ours as parents.

"Even many faithful Christians and their loved ones have bad things happen," said the Lord. "No one has the right to judge others, no matter what the situation is. But until you learn through your own experience, this is a hard truth to understand."

Day 68

Upon the Lord

I will love You, O LORD, *my strength. The* LORD *is my rock and my fortress and my deliverer; my God, my strength, in whom I will trust; my shield and the horn of my salvation, my stronghold. I will call upon the* LORD, *who is worthy to be praised; so shall I be saved from my enemies.*

—PSALM 18:1–3

After three and a half years with the Lord, I realize that my thoughts and actions are no longer my own. My entire life belongs to God.

My thinking, my feelings, and my behaviors all have changed, which I recognize with utmost humility. I have so much more compassion for lost and needy souls, and my heart aches for anyone who does not know the Lord.

Now I know that when I please my Lord and always put Him first, everything in my life will work out. My wonderful Lord has transformed me inside out, and He has taught me many amazing things about His ways.

No one can make me angry any longer because of the Lord's great love in my life.

Heavenly Father, may the compassion I feel for others, planted in my heart by You, grow to maturity and never fail to affect my motives, my motions, and my moments of care and concern . . .

Dear Father,
I pray that the urgency I feel in my own heart might be conveyed to others, that all might realize the imminence of your return and the eminence of Your domain over all that exists in the universe, including our immortal souls . . .

INTO THE SCHOOLS

And the Lord God of the holy prophets sent His angel to show His servants the things which must shortly take place.

—Revelation 22:6

"If the disobedient people don't wake up," the Lord said, "they will not hear the trumpet sound and they will have to go through the tribulation." He then went on to explain that He has been warning people through events related to school children, but that we have only feared Him for a short time before going back to our old ways.

"I have been giving them many signs to bring prayer back into the schools, but people are not really trying to do it. I will never force anyone. I can only give them signs so they will know what I want them to do.

"But I cannot wait forever for those who don't want to be ready for Me. I am coming for those who are ready for Me, and this will happen sooner than they expect."

The Lord said I must put these words in *Heaven Is So Real!*

Day 70

THE TRUMPET SOUND

When You did awesome things for which we did not look, You came down, the mountains shook at Your presence.

—ISAIAH 64:3

He reminded me that He has given people every chance to know Him. He has shown many signs to people to help them realize that He is God.

"But people do not fear Me, and many of those who know My words don't believe Me enough to live by My commandments. But I will give them another chance through your book and many other signs.

"Read Isaiah 64:3," He said. This prophetic passage talks about the mountains quaking at the Lord's presence.

"Whoever is ready for Me will hear the trumpet sound. I am coming for those who are ready for Me."

The Lord repeats many things. He wants so much for people to get ready for His coming.

Dear Jesus, I pray once again for increased awareness within the hearts and minds of all people, that the saved might be better aware of the lateness of the hour and that the unsaved might listen and heed Your voice . . .

Day 71

Heavenly Father, I pray for the anointing of the Lord, that I might always know when it is upon Your anointed ones, and that others might also sense it and allow Your presence to work in our midst . . .

DANCING IN THE SPIRIT

He was transfigured before them. His face shone like the sun, and His clothes became as white as the light.

—MATTHEW 17:2

The Lord has often repeated things to me. I'm sure this has been His way of making sure I understand and remember the important things. However, I had to go through many disappointments.

Now, the Lord directed me to put out my hands toward Him. Then He raised His right hand and said, "I release your work." He then explained to me that the day I began to dance, my ministry was released to the church. During each dance the Lord's presence is with me. Miracles abound wherever the Lord's presence is.

Several people have told me that they feel a special anointing when I dance. These are Spirit-filled people who know how to discern the work and presence of the Lord.

Day 72

DIVINE HEALING

If My people who are called by My name will humble themselves, and pray and seek My face, and turn from their wicked ways, then I will hear from heaven, and will forgive their sin and heal their land.

—2 CHRONICLES 7:14

Dearest Jesus, I pray for humility, both for myself and for others, that we might all worship You in full awareness of Your almighty presence and power, on which I depend for all my own strength . . .

Before I met my Lord Jesus, I had some emotional and physical problems. After about two months, every emotional problem I had previously experienced was healed and erased. For example, no matter how angry I would become I could no longer say any bad words.

I still have physical pains sometimes, but He always heals me—sometimes instantly; sometimes it takes time. I've learned that nothing is impossible for our Lord. I am totally dependent on Him because I know He will take care of me.

When the Lord doesn't heal me instantly I beseech Him until He brings it to pass. The Lord told me, "Persistent prayer is answered because those who believe actually expect to be healed by Me, so they continually ask until they receive."

He also told me, "Impatient prayer never will receive anything from Me." Those who don't know enough of God's words cannot have faith or patience to receive all His promises.

Day 73

THE VOICE OF GOD

Confess your trespasses to one another, and pray for one another, that you may be healed. The effective, fervent prayer of a righteous man avails much.

—JAMES 5:16

Almighty God, may the fervent prayer of my heart always be directed first toward You, in all situations, in all possible sincerity with all due praise, worship, and humility . . .

The first thing many Christians do when they are sick is go to the doctor, instead of casting the devil out, praying to the Father in the name of Jesus, searching their hearts to see if they have sin within them, and repenting. However, sometimes the Lord does lead us to a doctor.

It's important for us to hear and know the voice of God in these situations. However, it is sometimes very hard to understand what the Lord wants you to do. Always pray about it first and ask Him. Then, no matter what decision comes to your heart, if you have peace about it, it is of God.

If it is Satan's decision, your mind will be confused. God is always peace.

If you continually ask for whatever you need or want, sooner or later you will hear His voice, because you are depending on Him. That is why persistent prayer will always be answered.

Day 74

Purity of Touch

Let them praise His name in the dance: let them sing praises to Him with the timbrel and harp.
—Psalm 149:3

The Lord didn't allow me to do any church work during my training years. He continually told me to focus on Him and to keep praying for His promises to be fulfilled. The presence of the Holy Spirit began to fill me, anoint me, and surround me as I danced before the Lord.

He will not allow my hands to touch anybody's body to pray at such times of great anointing. When I've tried to touch others my hand would not do so. When I am anointed to dance, no one is permitted to touch my hands or body.

I actually long to put my hands on other people's bodies to pray for them. For now, however, when I pray for sick people it is from a distance. During such times of intercession, the anointing comes upon my body and I shake, as if my own body has become a substitute for the ill body of the person I'm praying for.

When this happens, I see the Lord's presence with that person.

Dear Lord, may all the service I desire to offer You be under Your divine direction and control, and thus acceptable to You in all ways at all times...

NEVER LUKEWARM

But the anointing which you have received from Him abides in you, and you do not need that anyone teach you; but as the same anointing teaches you concerning all things, and is true, and is not a lie, and just as it has taught you, you will abide in Him.

—1 JOHN 2:27

Dear Jesus, I pray that Your anointing would fall on me and never depart, that I might live continually, reborn and refreshed, in Your glorious presence . . .

Please don't be too comfortable with the world. Stay awake, for our Lord Jesus is coming for us. This could happen at any time. If you are continually disobedient and enjoy the world more than our Lord Jesus, you cannot expect to see His face.

If you are a lukewarm Christian, please pay special attention to what I'm saying. You cannot love anything or anyone more than our Lord Jesus who died for you. If a preacher tells you that all Christians who go to church will go to heaven, you'd better find another church.

When we are saved, the Lord expects us to pray continually and study the Bible. When you continually study and pray, then you will understand the Bible's teachings.

His anointing will teach you all things.

Day 76

TO GIVE WHAT IS HIS

"Bring all the tithes into the storehouse, that there may be food in My house, and try Me now in this," says the LORD *of hosts, "if I will not open for you the windows of heaven and pour out for you such blessing that there will not be room enough to receive it."*

—MALACHI 3:10

Those who tithe and give offerings live lives that are continually blessed in every area. Those who don't tithe, even though they go to church and do many things for God's work, often find that their lives are never really blessed. And they continually have problems.

The tithe is 10 percent of your gross pay. God doesn't need our money, but He wants every believer to bring the tithe to His house so the church can do God's work.

If you truly want to be with Jesus forever in heaven, pay close attention to what the Lord says. I have a responsibility to write the truth of God's words. I wrote this as clearly as I can so that new believers and some Christians who are confused about the tithe and offering can fully understand.

Father, I pray that all our tithes might be given gladly and that all might be gathered into Your storehouse to bless both ourselves and those in need, whom only You can know...

Number of the Beast

He was granted power to give breath to the image of the beast, that the image of the beast should both speak and cause as many as would not worship the image of the beast to be killed. He causes all, both small and great, rich and poor, free and slave, to receive a mark on their right hand or on their foreheads, and that no one may buy or sell except one who has the mark or the name of the beast, or the number of his name.... His number is 666.

—Revelation 13:15–18

Dear Father, may all my waking moments be given to You, to be used as You desire, especially for telling others about You as You so direct . . .

When I tell others about Jesus I often start by telling them what He did for us and how much He loves us. If they still refuse salvation, I tell them—if you are still alive after God's people are taken to heaven—never receive Satan's number, 666.

If you receive this number you will be with Satan, not Jesus, and you will burn in the lake of fire throughout eternity. If you refuse to receive Satan's number you may be killed, but you will live forever because you died for Jesus.

I believe the Holy Spirit leads me to say these things. That's why I have supernatural boldness to speak this message to others.

Day 78

MIRACULOUS DOINGS

[It is] He who supplies the Spirit to you and works miracles among you…

—GALATIANS 3:5

Suddenly I realized how many wrong things I had been doing for so long. Also, I had complained so many times about my discouragement. Immediately I began to humble myself before the Lord and ask forgiveness.

He softly replied, "I have forgotten all that." Then the Lord began to talk to me. "I have been saying to you that you must focus on your Lord first, then your work. You haven't been doing that.

"During every dance you are concerned about miracles for the people and you are forgetting your Lord's glory. This dance I created for My pleasure, not for you to be worrying about miracles.

"When I am pleased, then the miracles will happen. They are My miracles, not yours."

Dear Father, may I never forget that miracles, like simpler blessings, are Yours to give, Yours to bring about, Yours with which to glorify Yourself, and never mine or even about me…

Day 79

TO SPREAD THE WORD

Dear Jesus, I pray that all my efforts to witness to others might be fully directed by You, that I might never attempt to do Your work on my own power, but that when You direct me I might be fully responsive to Your leading...

For God so loved the world that He gave His only begotten Son, that whoever believes in Him should not perish but have everlasting life.

—JOHN 3:16

The vision of heaven that I have been so blessed to receive impels me to witness to others. I buy Bibles and New Testaments to give to others. I mark all the important passages, write notes to explain about Jesus, and include a tract about salvation. I give these out every time I have an opportunity to witness.

I talk to people everywhere—in grocery stores, parking lots, the mall, at the post office, and in waiting lines at banks. What a privilege it is to witness for my Lord wherever I go.

My desire to talk about Jesus is so overwhelming that I truly cannot help myself. Sometimes this is irritating to others who go with me; therefore, I usually go out alone.

I have learned that the best way for me to begin witnessing to someone is to simply ask if they believe in Jesus. Many will respond, "I believe in God." This usually means that they don't know anything about Jesus. Then I begin to present the gospel message.

Day 80

WE SEE IN PART

And it shall come to pass afterward that I will pour out My Spirit on all flesh; your sons and your daughters shall prophesy, your old men shall dream dreams, your young men shall see visions.

—JOEL 2:28

When we go to heaven, we will see two different valleys outside the gates of the kingdom. Those who find themselves in the valleys remain outside of the kingdom of heaven.

When we go into the kingdom of heaven it will be one thousand times better than this earth has been, even when we are walking here with our Lord Jesus. He has prepared all things for our pleasure, and He knows what we like!

Remember, almost all things in heaven are similar to what we have on earth. Yet the beauty of earth can never compare to heaven.

Some will say that they cannot believe these things because they are not in the Bible. That is a matter of personal choice. However, I have discovered that almost everything the Lord has shown me has its roots in the Bible. The Lord has chosen me for End-Times prophecy so He can show me things that are not clearly explained in the Bible

Almighty God, may all the valley dwellers in this world upgrade themselves by sincere acceptance of Your salvation and earnest pursuit of relationship with You, to rise one day from the depths of the valleys into heaven itself . . .

Day 81

FREELY GIVEN

For the poor will never cease from the land; therefore I command you, saying, "You shall open your hand wide to your brother, to your poor and your needy, in your land."

—DEUTERONOMY 15:11

O Jesus, may all of my resources be at Your service, ready at all times to be used as You command, for Your purposes . . .

Early one Saturday morning I stopped at a car wash and noticed a group of people on one side, who were very friendly. They were inviting people to talk about Russia and an evangelistic crusade that was coming soon. They were collecting offerings for the Russian church.

I had only $40 with me, but I immediately gave it to them. When I went home I felt a deep desire to give more. Suddenly I thought about the $500 in cash that I had saved for my own emergency use. So I asked the Lord, and He told me that I must give it.

When I returned to the car wash and gave the money to them, I felt very happy. After I got into the car I began to laugh with such joy that I couldn't stop laughing all the way home. The minute I walked into the house, I began laughing harder and jumping up and down with unspeakable joy.

I was so happy because I knew the Lord was happy. Ever since then He has blessed us more than we could have imagined.

Day 82

SPEAK UNTO OTHERS

But know this, that in the last days perilous times will come.

—2 TIMOTHY 3:1

As I have witnessed I have learned about people's workplaces. For example, if there are five people in the workplace and two of them are saved, in many cases the unsaved ones never hear about Jesus from the other two.

I know this often happens, because when I witness to the three who don't know about Jesus most of them are very glad to hear it. At that point they often say that they know their co-workers are Christians, but the Christians have never told the others about their faith.

We need to share our faith with all those we know, for witnessing is the most important work we can ever do for our Lord Jesus.

He died for sinners. I believe that it makes God unhappy when Christians don't talk about their salvation with unbelievers.

Our heavenly Father, I pray that I might never fail to witness for You when You present the opportunity; that I might be faithful, eager, and even bold in speaking of You as You direct...

Day 83

VIA NEW TONGUES

And these signs will follow those who believe: In My name they will cast out demons; they will speak with new tongues.

—MARK 16:17

One day the Lord said to me, "In your next prayer you will speak in a new tongue."

A couple of hours later I began to pray again. A special, fiery anointing came over my entire body. It turned out to be that new tongue that the Lord had given to me.

I have received various tongues many times before, but this one was a very long one. It required me to pray much longer than usual. I couldn't understand anything that I said, but the Lord told me not to be concerned. He assured me that He understands everything, and He told me that He is opening doors for every area of my ministry.

The Lord told me that from that day forward I would not be praying for those I had been praying for over such a long span of time. He said that I must pray only for my family, my pastor, and my church.

From then on I have been praying for others in my spare time rather than in my periods of regular prayer.

Dearest Father, may all Your gifts to me be on loan, used by me only to glorify You through righteous worship, praise, and adoration at the clear direction of the Holy Spirit...

THE VOICE OF GOD

Oh, clap your hands, all you peoples! Shout to God with the voice of triumph!

—PSALM 47:1

Some people think that because they can't hear God's voice He isn't listening or will not answer their prayers. At the beginning of my Christian walk I didn't know how to pray, and I never heard His voice.

But I was very persistent, and I believed I would receive what I requested from Him. I prayed many times a day. I asked the same things over and over, like a child. I needed so many things then. About two months later the Lord began to answer my prayers, one by one.

As a result, I began to fear God in a reverential way and to humble myself before Him. I learned to pray more often and began to read the Bible, even though I couldn't understand much of it. I began to make a habit of reading the Word and praying many times each day.

Dearest Jesus, I pray that I might always be persistent, whether I hear Your voice or not, knowing that You are always there, always listening, and always willing to guide, direct, and respond to Your children...

Day 85

He Loves Us More

Yet regard the prayer of Your servant and his supplication, O Lord my God, and listen to the cry and the prayer which Your servant is praying before You.

—2 Chronicles 6:19

Heavenly Father, may I never grow comfortable with my own comfort; may I never pass over into passivity or neglect to care—and pray—for others . . .

He shall cry to Me, "You are my Father, My God, and the rock of my salvation."

—Psalm 89:26

I was crying very hard and couldn't stop. A strong anointing of the Lord's presence came over me, and I noticed my Lord Jesus was crying with me.

"My coming for My people is so near. Satan knows this, and he is trying to destroy as many souls as he can before they are saved. People should realize why so many people are dying now. Every church must cast out the devil continually by prayer. My churches have been too comfortable.

"I love My children, and that is why I died for them. I must be first in everyone's life. Everyone needs to repent and be humble before Me. There will be a great distraction in this world continually until I come for My people. That day is sooner than they expect."

Our Lord Jesus loves us so much that He doesn't want anyone to miss the trumpet sound. He said no one can love Him more than He loves us. If I say to Him, "I love You a million, billion ways," He still says, "I love you more."

Day 86

BEFORE OUR ELDERS

Likewise you younger people, submit yourselves to your elders. Yes, all of you be submissive to one another, and be clothed with humility, for "God resists the proud, but gives grace to the humble."

—1 PETER 5:5

O Lord, like all others I have so much to be humble about. May I not dwell on my failures, but may I learn from and rise above them, and develop that deep humility so characteristic of our Lord and Savior, despite His awesome divinity . . .

Humility is so important to our Lord. He exemplified the importance of humility to us by humbling Himself to become a human being when He was in this world. I'm thankful to Him for showing and teaching me humility in so many ways.

I had been praying for humility, and still do, because I want to practice humility toward every human being. I want every aspect of my being to be like Jesus. No matter what the situation may be, I never want to judge others. I want to love them and pray for them. That is what our Lord desires from each of us.

After a heavenly vision, the Lord gave me a great desire to read 1 Corinthians 13. I have been reading it six days a week, and I have never missed reading it yet, but I never try to memorize it.

I believe the Lord put His love into my spirit through His words. The Lord also gave me a desire to pray the Lord's Prayer every day after my regular prayer.

Dear Father, please help me to develop humility and patience, knowing that these are both divine attributes that set Your people apart from the world . . .

A GOD OF ORDER

And God has appointed these in the church: first apostles, second prophets, third teachers, after that miracles, then gifts of healings, helps, administrations, varieties of tongues.

—1 CORINTHIANS 12:28

He could have healed me instantly as He had so many other times before, but this time He was teaching me humility before Him in public. It is very hard for some people to humble themselves before the Lord at the altar or in public.

Yes, it is very important to the Lord that His people be humble before Him and before others. I have experienced this while praising the Lord in my seat and at the altar. The difference is that I can feel Holy Spirit fire hit me each time I kneel before the Lord.

When we belong fully to our Lord Jesus, we must not worry about what people will say or think. The most important thing is pleasing our Lord.

The Essence of Salvation

And do this, knowing the time, that now it is high time to awake out of sleep; for now our salvation is nearer than when we first believed. The night is far spent, the day is at hand. Therefore let us cast off the works of darkness, and let us put on the armor of light.

—Romans 13:11–12

The Lord reminded me to write about people who claim to be saved but never go to church or participate with other Christians. Some people think that being baptized with water is what saves them. The Lord told me that the only ones who are truly saved are those who live according to His commandments and walk in His Holy Spirit.

Whoever believes in Him must love Him with their whole heart and have fellowship with other Christians. God also expects them to attend church and pay their tithes and offerings. Those who are unable to attend church must give their tithes and offerings to the local church, or any other church.

Jesus said, "Anyone who is saved must share My words with others and worship Me with others as one unit. Also, those who are unable to go to church must pray for the pastors and churches, and pray for the salvation of the lost."

Dearest Jesus, I pray for all those who assume salvation but do not truly know You, that their hearts might be awakened and their minds quickened, to cast themselves totally on Your personal mercies rather than rituals and ceremonies...

Day 89

SALVATION!

Jesus said to him, "I am the way, the truth, and the life. No one comes to the Father except through Me."

—John 14:6

Father in heaven, I pray that all who come to You might come in the name of Your beloved Son, Jesus Christ, for whom there simply is no substitute . . .

I have heard many people say that they believe in God but don't believe in Jesus. Please believe what I am saying. Even if you believe in God and you don't believe that Jesus is the Son of God, there is no salvation.

Jesus is the only one who can save you and forgive all your sins so you can have eternal life with Him. (See Mark 9:48.) If you have never before asked Jesus to save you, now is the time for you to do so.

Simply say this prayer aloud, from your heart:

> Lord Jesus, I believe You are the Son of God and You died for me. Please come into my heart, be my Lord and Savior, forgive me of all my sins, and take control of every area of my life from this moment on. Jesus, fill me with Your Holy Spirit and use me for Your glory. I want to serve You and love You all the days of my life. Thank You, Father, that I am now Your child, in Jesus' holy name. Amen.

After this prayer, to work out your salvation, read the Bible, pray continually, and go to church to listen to God's words and fellowship with God's people. Your life will never be the same; you'll have a very happy life while on this earth and live forever with Jesus in heaven. God bless you.

IN CLOSING...

I will stand my watch and set myself on the rampart, and watch to see what He will say to me, and what I will answer when I am corrected. Then the LORD answered me and said: "Write the vision and make it plain on tablets, that he may run who reads it. For the vision is yet for an appointed time; but at the end it will speak, and it will not lie. Though it tarries, wait for it; because it will surely come, it will not tarry."

—HABAKKUK 2:1–3

At this juncture I ask only that you receive this book in the same way it was written—with total openness to the Lord and His will. I again invite you to evaluate my experiences in the light of the Word of God.

At the Lord's direction, I have done as the Old Testament prophet Habakkuk did—I have watched and waited for Him to see what He would say to me.

Like Habakkuk, I have written my vision down and made it plain, so that you who read it may "run" according to the Lord's perfect plan for you—a plan that includes a place already prepared for you in heaven if you only will believe in His Son and receive Him as your personal Lord and Savior.

For surely He is coming soon!

Father, I look for Your Son's return to take us away to be with You forever. O, how I long for that day! Until then, may I boldly proclaim the name of Jesus to everyone I meet. Even so, Lord Jesus, come!

JOURNAL

What ministry has God called you to for these End Times? What kinds of preparations has He been making in you—physically, socially, financially, and the like—to achieve His purposes in you?

JOURNAL

SCRIPTURE KEYS FOR HOLY LIVING

God loves you very much, and I hope that these verses of faith, healing, truth, and love will allow you to experience—as I have many times—the presence of our beloved Savior, Jesus Christ.

—CHOO THOMAS
WWW.CHOOTHOMAS.COM

You are healed by the stripes of Christ. See Isaiah 53:5.

Those who have pure hearts will see God. See Matthew 5:8.

Your heavenly Father sees your *humble* deeds and will reward you. See Matthew 6:1–6.

Take the narrow road. It leads to life. See Matthew 7:13–14.

God knows those who do His will. See Matthew 7:21–23.

Separate from anything that causes you to sin. See Mark 9:43–48.

The greatest thing you can do is love God and love others. See Mark 12:30–31.

Give God first place in your life. See Luke 14:26–27.

Your obedience shows your love for God. See John 14:15–24.

You will go through trials on your way to the kingdom. See Acts 14:22.

Not one thing in this life will separate you from God's love. See Romans 8:35.

Jesus works to present you holy and pure before Him. See Ephesians 5:27.

Obey God with deep reverence and holy fear. See Philippians 2:12.

God will be seen in you as you walk in peace and holiness. See Hebrews 12:14.

You are healed and made righteous through Christ's sacrifice on the cross. See 1 Peter 2:24.

Rest in God's care, and be strengthened by faith in His Word. See 1 Peter 5:6–9.

Read this every day, and watch God's heart of love overtake you day by day. See 1 Corinthians 13.

Build an eternal foundation that cannot be consumed by fire. See 1 Corinthians 3:12–15.

You are held accountable for the things you do on earth, whether good or bad. See 2 Corinthians 5:10.